Person and Character Level Life Coaching and Mentoring

Life Coaching and Mentoring from an Expanded Paradigm

Dr. Dennis Morgan

Person and Character Level Life Coaching and Mentoring
by Dr. Dennis Morgan.
Copyright © 2017 by Dr. Dennis Morgan. All rights reserved.
ISBN: 978-0-9982118-2-4

Graphics & Layout: OM EAST, Spillern, Austria.
Bible quotations are from the English Standard Version.
Dr. Morgan can be contacted at: personlifecoach@gmail.com

Table of Contents

The Why and What of Person and Character Level Life Coaching and Mentoring

There are numerous good books about life coaching, so why write another one? One reason would be if a different paradigm was being introduced – an expanded understanding as the base for a model of change for life coaching. How much different or distinct could a paradigm be in this day and age? If the *starting point* and the *primary focus* were shifted to a different level, one that is distinct, would that qualify? I believe it would qualify as an expanded paradigm if the person is understood to be distinct from, yet integrated with the physical body and if the functioning of the person is not viewed as primarily psychological, but rather related to character.

The person as distinct from the body and functioning as related to character, make this book unique in both its *starting point* and its *primary focus*. First, the *starting point* or ground upon which this approach is based is a structural view of human nature that is informed by psychological and philosophical ideas and a theological perspective. Taking life coaching and mentoring into an expanded paradigm includes change not only at the usual personal and situational level, but also involves change at a deeper level – the level of the person who is defined as being a soul. Establishing an understanding of the immaterial soul as the person and then utilizing this to assist others in making positive change, points to the *primary focus*: virtues and character. Though psychological issues and psychological functioning are important, they are not the primary focus for change. Rather, the primary focus is on the person making progress in virtue development that then translates into character-based choices affecting the whole person. This is an approach to and model of life coaching that is distinct. As well, there are definite advantages in this expanded model with regard to persons: being able to detach from problems (self-distancing) and having confidence in their ability to succeed in making personal changes (self-efficacy).

The clarified view of the soul as the conscious person who is experiencing life in a physical body, along with the emphasis on virtue or character development, is a paradigm expansion. Life coaching that does not include these dimensions of understandings is at one level of change – addressing situational and psychological issues of the whole person. The distinction of the soul-person from the brain (and body) and the strengthening of character to increase personal coping and resilience, expands life coaching and mentoring. Including these dimensions of understanding allows for a new level of depth in a life coaching and mentoring model of change.

The material in this book is a combination of two separate but integrated works. They are being presented here together for convenience and for clarification. With regard to convenience, some individuals will be interested in understanding both the overall model of life coaching and the introductory level training in life mentoring. They are together here, so that only one volume is needed to accomplish this understanding.

This combined work is also being done for the purpose of clarification. Although the *Life Coaching Basics*[1] book material is being placed first here, it is not chronologically first in the sequence of training. *An Introduction to Life Mentor Training*[2] is the foundational, entry level of training for lay people, with the move to learning life coaching coming later, after their life mentoring supervised practice experience. Why then have *Life Coaching Basics* first? It is because the model of care is developed and explained in *Life Coaching Basics*. This then is the logical starting point. *An Introduction to Life Mentor Training* follows it in order to elaborate on concepts and to demonstrate an approach to training that culminates in being a person and character level life coach.

---

[1]   Morgan, D. D. (2016). *Life Coaching Basics*. Spillern, Austria: OM EAST.
[2]   Morgan, D. D. (2016). *An introduction to Life MentorTtraining*. Spillern, Austria: OM EAST.

While reading the material in this book, it will become evident that there is an overlap and duplication between *Life Coaching Basics* and *An Introduction to Life Mentor Training*. No attempt has been made to minimize this. Rather the material for each book is left in its original form so that the integration of the two can be seen. Person and character level life mentoring is a valuable means for offering support, but it is not the end state for training. Person and character level life coaching is the full preparation for a person and character level approach to helping others make positive changes in their lives from the depth of the soul-person.

Here are brief summaries of what each of the books is addressing.

BOOK 1: *Life Coaching Basics* presents advanced concepts for assisting others who are experiencing personal struggles. It is grounded in an understanding that the immaterial soul is the real person who animates the whole person. This real person is who the life coach encourages toward more effective personal coping, resilience, and flourishing. Life coaching builds on the skills of life mentoring, by adding deeper level understandings of psychological processes. Life coaches are more highly skilled in assisting others and are focused on positive, non-psychological goals for personal change.

BOOK 2: *An Introduction to Life Mentor Training* presents a model for training life mentors to effectively assist others who are experiencing personal struggles. It introduces an approach to life mentoring that is grounded in an understanding that the immaterial soul is the real person. This real person is the one who animates the whole person and is who the life mentor encourages toward more effective personal coping, resilience, and flourishing. Life mentors focus on positive, non-psychological goals for personal change.

As mentioned previously, **BOOK 1:** *Life Coaching Basics* though not the chronological place to begin training individuals, is the logical place to begin understanding this person and character level life coaching model of change. The Ten Tasks defined within this book summarize both the key elements in this approach to life coaching, as well as the way that the process unfolds and repeats. BOOK 1 has to be understood in its entirety in order for the expanded paradigm for life coaching and mentoring to make sense.

BOOK 1:
Life Coaching Basics

Introduction

Life Coaching Basics is focused on specific topics that are particularly significant for providing personal life coaching. It has been compiled as the result of having taught and revised and re-taught the Life Mentor Training, as well as having done individual and group supervision with life mentors-in-training. Hearing their reactions has shaped my thinking about what is needed for the next level of training — training for life coaches. This material has incorporated what has emerged as being both basic and necessary for doing life coaching well. *Life Coaching Basics* builds upon the foundation of Life Mentor Training material.[1]

Life coaching is a real, helping relationship with another person. It is different from doing counseling or psychotherapy, but shares a similar reason for deciding to help: a situation is causing a personal struggle. Due to the other's personal issues and suffering, there is not only a need to assist the person to be able to cope better now, but there is also the need to prevent these issues from interfering with life flourishing. Life coaching is on the same continuum of helping as life mentoring, but goes beyond life mentoring. Life coaching adds a deeper level of understanding of a client's psychological processes and allows for more assisting in managing these processes, while staying focused on non-psychological change goals. As well, life coaching further defines the important components of life coaching meetings.

Life coaching shares with life mentoring the **three primary life goals**. The first two are easily understood and affirmed. **First**, life coaching works to strengthen the here and now (real-time) relationship the other person has with God.[2] **Secondly**, life coaching

---

[1] Morgan, *An Introduction to Life Mentor Training*.

[2] Life coaching is offered both for people who consciously identify themselves as Christian and also for those who do not identify as consciously Christian. The goals are similar for both, with a distinction in the first goal: **First**, life coaching works to strengthen the here and now (real-time) relationship the other person has with God or with reference to a higher power.

encourages growth in character (virtue development). However, reaching these two primary goals leads to accomplishing *a desired third goal*: improved personal coping and resilience. In other words, life coaching seeks to effectively assist in bringing about, through improved relating with God and increased character formation, enhanced personal functioning. The individual is thus enabled to better manage and transcend personal life issues and challenges.

To accomplish these goals, life coaches help clients move through *three stages of change*. The first stage is *Telling Their Story*. The second stage is *Setting Situational Goals*. The final stage is *Taking Action*. The character-based quality of the relationship between the life coach and the client is the powerful context for change.

These goals and stages are a foundational part of the basic structure of life coaching, but they are not the most foundational or the only important pieces. Even more foundational is a well-developed view of how humans are constructed. This will be described in the section Basic 1. Following that material will be a discussion of the process of life coaching. Subsequent Basic sections will give explanations to concepts and resources that have surfaced as being relevant and necessary for life coaches to understand and know how to use. Basic 9 pulls all the other Basic topics together to provide a composite picture of how life coaching is done.

BASIC 1: Being Human

For many of us there is a big disconnect between what we experience internally about our persons and what we have been taught to believe. When I am aware of myself, I seem to be a person who exists and will always exist. I live in a body, but I don't seem to just be a body. In school science classes, I was taught that people evolved from matter, and the message was that the physical body is all that there really is. This didn't fit with my experience of myself, but of course, who would I have been to argue with science?

I was taught that people evolved from matter,
and the message was that the
physical body is all that there really is.

Then there is spiritual teaching. I feel like I exist and there is teaching that I am more than my body. However, if the teaching declares that God created me soul and body, is that enough explanation? What about my everyday experience of being more than my body and even more than that part of my body that is my brain? What does the spiritual teaching say about how to be a spirit being? Does a spiritual perspective explain not only the existence of a soul or spirit within a body, but also my experience of my person as being distinct from my brain and body?

We want to live-out our desires to be a growing, developing, progressing person. However, even when we focus on what we desire for ourselves, we're not always able to do it, often because something inside of us interferes with reaching our goals. We have deep desires about what we want to be, but the challenge is to make it happen.

Life coaches can help other people reach their personal goals and flourish. However, to adequately help another person requires having a clear understanding of persons. This understanding involves knowing how people are structured internally, the human nature. Information on the topic of human nature is a necessary starting place for understanding ourselves and others — for getting further acquainted with who humans really are.

Illustrations About Human Natures

Mapping-out the terrain of our inner life (human nature) is difficult and abstract.[3] For our purposes, I will simply provide two illustrations that will hopefully make the structure of human nature more understandable. One illustration is from fantasy and one is from actual history. Let's keep in mind that when we are talking about human nature, we are talking about the person and the body and their relationship.

Here's the illustration from a fantasy comic book character. Concerning human nature, our person is to our brain and body as perhaps Tony Stark is to his Iron Man suit. (If you're not familiar with the Iron Man movie, there's a link below for an Iron Man [Suit Up] film clip[4]) The super hero character, Tony Stark, built a suit that had certain capabilities, including a computer that Tony could interact with from within the suit. But make-no-mistake, Tony was the person animating the suit. When the illustration is understood this way, one can more clearly visualize the idea that the-person-is-not-the-same-as the brain and body. It is true, in the movie, that Tony and the suit are in some sense one, but they are also not one and the same. Tony and the suit become one, but Tony is always distinct from the suit and can always override what the suit and what its computer are doing.

---

[3]   I don't think most people are very interested in technical explanations, but for those who are, I've included more detailed information in Appendix A.

[4]   Iron Man YouTube film clip: "Iron Man: Suit up", Cinema Stars Official, accessed September 5, 2016 https://www.youtube.com/watch?v=Fcm7OjoOz4A.

The same is true for us; our persons (souls) and our bodies (including the brain) are distinct, but not separate. The soul is the person animating the functioning of the body. Similarly, when Tony was in the suit, he animated it — the suit came-to-life. When he was out of the suit, it was not alive, though the functions of the computer could still be run. You, your soul or person, animates your body and when you leave your body, your body is dead. A medical team could artificially keep your bodily functions going, but they cannot give a truly dead body life again. Only the presence of your soul, your person, gives life to your body.[5]

You, your soul or person, animates your body and when you leave your body, your body is dead.

The other illustration I offer is from the actual history of the Old Testament. The Israelites worshipped God in a temple. The design of the temple provides another illustration of how we are both soul and body that function together.

Solomon's Temple, in Diagram 1 below, was a complex that was divided into areas and rooms. The most inner part of the temple was the Holy of Holies where God would be present. Then there was the Holy Place where the priests typically presided. Outside those rooms was the Inner Court and beyond that the Outer Court.

---

[5] Morgan, *The Soul That Suffers* (2013) develops this view of human nature and combines it with information on suffering, specifically for use when counseling Christians.

Diagram 1: Solomon's Temple that was in Jerusalem.

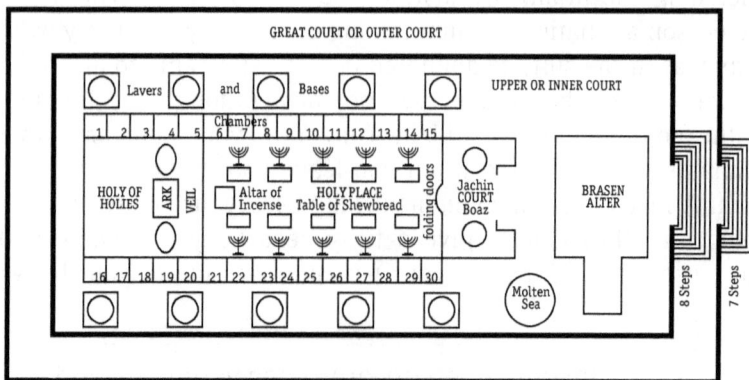

GREAT COURT OR OUTER COURT

| Lavers | and | Bases | | UPPER OR INNER COURT |

Chambers

1 2 3 4 5 6 7 8 9 10 11 12 13 14 15

HOLY OF HOLIES | ARK | VEIL | Altar of Incense | HOLY PLACE Table of Shewbread | folding doors | Jachin COURT Boaz | BRASEN ALTER

16 17 18 19 20 21 22 23 24 25 26 27 28 29 30

Molten Sea

8 Steps   7 Steps

The illustration works like this (see Diagram 2 below). The Holy of Holies is like the place within us that is the soul-person. The Holy Place represents the brain and the Inner Court the rest of the body. The only way out of the Holy of Holies was through the Holy Place and there was access between the Holy Place and the Inner Court. You can see the comparison with our whole person. The "way out of" our soul or person (that is, the way for the soul to be expressed) is through the brain, and there is then access between the physical brain and the rest of the physical body.[6]

The "way out of" our soul or person (that is, the way for the soul to be expressed) is through the brain.

---

[6]   Indications of the soul and brain-body reality are seen in Frankl's concept that the body and psyche unity, along with the essential ground of the spiritual core person, form a three-fold wholeness that makes man complete. Frankl, *The Unconscious God*, 28-29.

Diagram 2: The Whole-Person: Non-Physical Soul-Person and the Physical Brain and Body

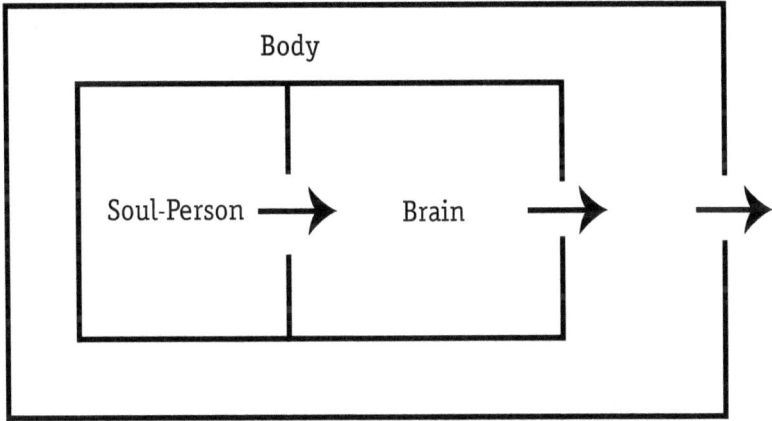

```
┌─────────────────────────────────────────────────────┐
│                      Body                             │
│   ┌─────────────────────────────────┐                 │
│   │                │                │                 │
│   │ Soul-Person ──▶    Brain     ──▶ │            ──▶  │
│   │                │                │                 │
│   └─────────────────────────────────┘                 │
│                                                       │
└─────────────────────────────────────────────────────┘
```

When you experience yourself as a person within a body, these two illustrations can be remembered. Hopefully, you will be able to break free of the confines of a narrow-minded view that there is no such thing as an immaterial soul that inhabits the body. The reality of being a soul, a person who makes the brain and body alive, will give you greater clarity about who you are and more freedom to make choices about how you want to live.[7]

---

[7]   The condition of the immaterial person is related to the degree of potential for making choices. There are two conditions: unregenerate and regenerate (see Appendix A for more details). God has not supernaturally changed the persons of unregenerate people. God supernaturally regenerates (re-creates) the immaterial persons of some individuals – being born again. So, the condition of one who is truly a Christian is one in which the immaterial person: has a will freed from the power of sin, has new godly desires (virtuous) that grow, and is empowered by the indwelling of the Holy Spirit. Regenerate individuals are already perfect in their persons, while still having not-yet redeemed brains and bodies, hence the continued occurrence of personal problems and sin. Their whole persons continue to struggle, in this life, both differently and in some ways similarly to those who are not regenerate (see Basic 8).

Summary Points

1. Human Beings have both material (brain and the rest of the body) and immaterial (the soul or actual person) parts to the whole person.

2. The soul animates and exerts influence over the brain and the rest of the body.

3. This view of the soul is essential for understanding life coaching's intention to align with the dominant or determinate will of the soul of the client in order to influence the psychological will of the brain – a process of a healthy detachment of the person from his or her problems.

BASIC 2: Life Coaching as a Process

There are stages of change in the overall process of life coaching. These same stages are happening in each meeting with a client and perhaps repeating more than once in the same meeting. One image of the repeating stages is a Russian Nesting Doll. Within each doll is another similar doll. Using this image, one can consider that within the overall stages, across all the meetings, are similar smaller occurrences of the stages in each meeting.

The following stages are repeated in each meeting:

1. *Telling Their Story* – **Current Picture**[8]

2. *Setting Situational Goals*[9] – **The Preferred Picture**

3. *Taking Action* – **The Way Forward**

In the **Current Picture** stage, you are helping clients tell their story – the overall story and the stories that they bring to each meeting. You are allowing them to disclose their thoughts, ideas, feelings, and struggles.

Within the overall stages, across all
the meetings, are similar smaller occurrences
of the stages in each meeting.

---

[8] Egan, *The skilled helper: A Problem-Management and Opportunity-Development Approach to Helping*.

[9] Please see Appendix B for clarifications regarding the simultaneous use of both *life goals* and *situational goals*.

Regarding **The Preferred Picture**, you are helping clients set viable situational goals for the overall coaching and within each meeting goals. These there are related to the clients' personally disclosed story. You can help identify goals from what they have disclosed.

The final stage that needs to happen is **The Way Forward**. This involves helping clients make some decisions about what actions to do. In other words, helping clients develop strategies and actions to accomplish their goals. It should be fairly obvious what clients have been doing that isn't working, but it is also helpful to know what they have tried that has provided some success.

Ten Tasks: How to Lead a Life Coaching Meeting

Another way to consider the life coaching process is to identify the various important tasks that should be intentionally incorporated into each life coaching meeting. These tasks are specific repeating components within the life coaching process. The components are being introduced here as the Ten Tasks and will be discussed more fully in the section Basic 9.

1. Begin the meeting with, "What's most important for you to talk about today?"

2. Actively listen to the *story* (Basic 2) using the life coach *attitudes* (Basic 3).

3. Understand what clients want and set *situational goals* (Basic 2).

4. Find out what stands in the way of reaching the situational goals, such as shifting client *parts* or modes (see Basic 5).

5. Explore, with clients, for their *deepest desires* (person-centered godly and positive goals − Basic 2) related to the story.

6. Agree on practical *action* (Basic 2) steps to reach goals.

7. Identify the related *virtues* (see Basic 4) that need to be strengthened.

8. Provide an explanation about God's *here and now* involvement in their story or how their higher power can be of benefit.

9. Remind clients about using *detachment* (see Basic 6) – that their persons can manage their brains and bodies.

10. As needed, *teach* clients about and *model* for them the life coaching concepts and process, especially whenever they seem confused and unclear.

A Final Reminder

Remember, if you jump to telling clients what they need to do before they have more fully told their story or before it has been determined what they want (goals), then you are likely slipping into advice giving, fixing, and taking inappropriate responsibility (a form of control). The decision about what clients need to do should flow naturally from the work done in the meeting, as shaped and influenced also by you.[10]

---

[10] A common solution offered by theologically conservative Christians, when a Christian is struggling with a personal problem, is that the person needs to identify and stop the sin. It may be true that some aspect or expression of the problem involves sin or the potential for sin. However, just because that is true does not mean that this truth alone will be helpful for knowing what steps to take to change. The Bible is intensive on the topics it covers, in that these topics are clearly explained, but it is not extensive in covering all areas of life. For example, in Romans 6:12 the Apostle Paul tells his readers to not let sin reign in their mortal bodies, but he does not tell them a specific set of steps to do in order to carry-out this imperative. Of course, for example, prayer would be an important spiritual intervention. Prayer is a specific behavior, but it is not an instruction in a process that the person could directly participate in for change and use to cooperate with the Holy Spirit. A psychological intervention could be helpful and used by God to bring about change. One might think this intervention to not be spiritual, but it may actually accomplish exactly the spiritual outcome Paul desired for his readers. One could then say that the psychological intervention was actually a spiritual means.

BASIC 3: Life Coach Attitudes and Relationship

Life coaching has a relationship focus for helping clients change. In this relationship, virtues are being communicated both by example (modeled) and by being directly taught.[11] In order for this exchange of virtues to be accomplished, certain core conditions have to be present in the relationship. These attitudes or core conditions have been widely researched.[12] The following is a description of these three basic attitudes or principles that reflect the attitude of the life coach toward the client.[13]

> In order for this exchange of virtues to be accomplished, certain core conditions have to be present in the relationship.

Attitudes (The Core Conditions)

1. **Congruence**: The life coach is congruent with the client. Congruence is also called genuineness. This means that life coaches are concerned to allow clients to experience them as they really are. The life coach does not have a facade, that is, the life coach's internal and external experiences are one in the same. In short, the life coach is authentic.

---

[11] When teaching my counseling graduate students empathy skills, I would remind them of Colossians 3:12-14 where the Apostle Paul describes virtues that are important interpersonally and particularly if one desires to be empathetic.

[12] "...the value of empathy, unconditional positive regard, and congruence is supported by the latest generation of psychotherapy process-outcome research." Kirschenbaum, *The Current Status of Carl Rogers and The Person-Centered Approach*, 46.

[13] This material is excerpted and adapted from: Saul McLeod, "Person Centered Therapy". (2015) www.simplypsychology.org/client-centred-therapy.html Accessed 5 September 2016

2. **Positive Regard**: The life coach provides the client with positive regard. It is believed that for people to grow and fulfill their potential it is important that they are valued as themselves. This refers to the life coach's deep and genuine caring for the client. The life coach may not approve of some of the client's actions, but the life coach does show acceptance toward the client's person. In short, the life coach needs an attitude of, "I'll accept you as you are." The life coach is thus careful to maintain a genuine positive attitude toward the client, even when in disagreement with the client's actions. (Note: Some client behavior and attitudes may need to be confronted, but timing and approach are crucial. The point here is for the life coach to not immediately become moralistic.)

3. **Empathy**: The life coach shows empathetic understanding to the client. Empathy is the ability to understand what the client is feeling. This refers to the life coach's ability to understand sensitively and accurately (but not sympathetically) the client's experience and feelings in the here-and-now. Empathy is understanding "as if" it were the life coach's experience, while not owning or taking-on the experience as one's own.

An important part of the task of the life coach is to follow precisely what the client is feeling and to communicate to the client that the life coach understands what the client is feeling.

Relationship

The horizontal or person-to-person dynamic life coaching relationship, well-supplied with virtue modeling and exchanges, is intended to be a bridge to the enhancement of the quality of the client's moment by moment (real-time) relationship with God as life is happening. This virtue-in-relationships approach to encouraging spiritual development is also expected to result in client improvements in life management and flourishing.

> This virtue-in-relationships approach to encouraging spiritual development is also expected to result in client improvements in life management and flourishing.

In the life coaching relationship, the client:

- Experiences the quality of character of the life coach.

- Learns about the needed virtues.

- Is encouraged to be active in the development of character.

- Is moved toward a closer, real-time (here and now) relationship with God or improved utilization of the higher power.

The life coach in relationship with clients:

- Listens as the clients tell their stories.

- Does not deny the psychological and emotional issues and pain.

- Chooses to help through the strengthening of character virtues.

- Lives-out character virtues in life coaching.

- Points clients to the means of receiving grace from God or improved utilization of the higher power.

- Encourages clients in practicing spiritual disciplines and virtues.

- Refers clients for psychological help when it is needed.

Summary Points

1. Life coaching addresses the soul and the functioning of the soul's character virtues, by providing a real relationship that models a healthy caring relationship and demonstrates Christ-like virtues..

2. The expectation is that sinful dispositions in the brain (and rest of the body) will weaken as the soul's virtues are strengthened and real-time relating with God improves.

3. Through the experience and practice of character virtues and real-time reliance on God, it is expected that eventually problems with personality functioning will become more contained and better managed.

BASIC 4: Building the Character Foundation

An Exchange of Virtues

There are those times in conversations when, as we are listening to another, there is this almost mystical experience of touching the heart (soul) of another. The topic might be about a relationship or a work situation or a decision or some other situation, but in these moments an exchange happens between persons (souls). I'm not talking necessarily about an intense emotional moment, but emotions are involved. It's more like getting our understanding of another communicated from who we are deep in our souls, to the deep soul level of the other – real person to real person. These are crucial moments of feeling loved by another in a particularly personal, yet in a respectful, intentional, and non-intrusive manner.

These are relational moments in which the care and character of one person is being communicated to another. This happens during conversations in which there is an exchange of information – listening to and speaking with a friend in need – with one as the supporter and one as a person being supported, or one as the life coach and one as a client who is being coached. Yet, at another level the one listening and supporting or coaching is a person who is being patient, gracious, kind – being caring and loving. These character qualities or virtues are being experienced and received by the other person and this other person resonates with these virtues – there is a virtue *exchange*. The exchange of virtues is not mystical, except in the sense that what is happening might not be well understood. It is important for life coaches to understand this exchange and the human context in which it happens.

Life coaching is a way to improve the resilience of the person to life challenges, such that there is improved personal functioning. This is accomplished through a relationship in which virtues are encouraged, as is a deepening relationship with God. Even though the life coaching focus is on character development and not directly on psychological factors, improved personal functioning is also an outcome.

These character qualities or virtues are being
experienced and received by the other person
and this other person resonates with
these virtues – there is a virtue exchange.

On Virtue and Character Development

Life coaching is a different way of thinking about how to assist others. Virtues and a relationship with God often operate in the background of life.[14] More obvious are the problems in living and the focus on more concrete and common sense solutions that are action-oriented. If a person is depressed, for example, then the solution appears to be to directly change the depression. However, we know that a complete operational goal is not to merely reduce to depression, because that is taking away a negative without replacing it with a positive. The obvious positive solution is to increase the person's joy in living, possibly through increased pleasurable activities and/or increasing positive interactions with others. What is missing even in this is the reality that it takes character qualities or virtues, as the foundation to these solutions, in order for the person to be able to practice or perform them. However, if instructed about the presence of and characteristics of virtues and the consequent actions connected to virtues, then clients become aware of and can be encouraged to identify virtues in their own internal lives that have always been operating, influencing emotional and relational living. The life coaching strengthening of the soul's character virtues, that results in enhanced personality functioning, is somewhat analogous to what physical therapy does in strengthening surrounding muscles, in order to compensate for an injured muscle and to prevent further loss of and promote improvement in functioning.

---

[14] The Apostle Peter, in 2 Peter 1:5-9, expresses the importance of increasing in virtues.

One could consider love to be the overarching virtue in life coaching, because the quality of the client's virtue of love is critical for the quality of the client's character and the quality of the client's real-time relationship with God. The "quality of the client's character" refers to the virtues present in the client and how well-developed and practically applied those virtues are for daily living. In other words, the client's ability to function and flourish in life, amid its many challenges is directly associated with how developed and operational are the virtues held within the person and from the person toward others. Virtues are directly connected with personal functioning and flourishing in life. To live with underdeveloped character, by contrast, is to not have character virtues as an established resource to engage with life and to be more fully and positively present in relationships.

> The life coaching strengthening of the
> soul's character virtues, that results in
> enhanced personality functioning, is somewhat
> analogous to what physical therapy does
> in strengthening surrounding muscles.

What is meant by the phrase, "the quality of the client's real-time relationship with God?" A real-time relationship refers to the how well clients are able, in the here and now, to connect with the loving presence of God in the activities of the outward life and in the processes of the inward life. To have a real-time relationship with God is to have a dynamic loving relationship with God as life is lived. This dynamic (active, changing, responsive, and progressing[15]) loving relationship is the immediate involvement and interaction of God with the person. The stronger the person's virtues are, particularly the virtue of love, the more deeply and strongly intimate will be the connection in real-time relating.

---

[15] Please do not misunderstand this comment to be saying that God is changing or evolving in response to us. God's essence is unchanging.

As the virtue of love increases, clients are more able to hold the reality of God's existing in the present time and being actively engaged with them, even though God is invisible and not heard as an audible voice. This type of connection with God should not be too much to imagine for the person who has the ability to hold internal representations of loved ones, even while apart from these loved ones. The connection with the loved one is "experienced" even though not physically present. The person has the ability to bring the physically absent loved one into current situations and internal processes in a relationally dynamic manner. The client should, in other words, be able to believe and trust intellectually and emotionally that the loved ones affection, commitment, understanding, and other dimensions of relationship are really present. With God there is an added reality to this type of connection, because unlike the absent loved one, God is really present everywhere, at all times, and to the same extent, and He is responsive.

When considering this immediate and constant experiencing of relationship with God, questions may arise about whether God relates in real-time. However, this intimate way of God relating with people is biblically documented in Jesus' interactions with people. There are recorded accounts of actual person-to-person interactions that Jesus had with individuals (e.g., with the Samaritan woman at the well, the woman caught in the act of adultery, or Peter in the reinstatement after betraying Jesus). In life coaching, the client is encouraged to be open to God's personal, powerful, good, and loving relating in the here and now. The client's necessary personal condition, for receiving and resonating with a real-time relationship with the Lord, is a progressively growing quality of character. Virtues consistent with the character of God are necessary for a fuller and deeper intimacy in a relationship with God. In other words, the more similarity in character with Christ, the more this real-time relationship will flourish.

Virtues consistent with the character of God
are necessary for a fuller and deeper
intimacy in a relationship with God.

Life coaches can point their clients toward ways to increase their virtues. For those who identify as being Christians, spiritual disciplines can be practiced such as prayer and reading of scripture, as well as solitude, silence, fasting, serving others, and confession. These would be human cooperative efforts to increase in virtues. Ultimately, the source of virtue development is understood to be the Holy Spirit.

Summary Points

1. Virtues are understood to reside within the soul, who is the real person, though being expressed through the rest of the person (brain and body).

2. Virtues are believed to be present in all people as a part of the image of God.

3. Virtues can grow and the potential for growth is greater for Christians, whose souls have been regenerated, freed from the power of sin, and who have the Holy Spirit's illuminating and strengthening at work within them.

BASIC 5: Seeing the Shifting Psychological Parts

Descriptions and Definitions of Parts or Modes

One of the challenges in our own responses to situations is that we react out of parts of our psychological selves. You might have thought to yourself or said to someone, "a part of me wants to _____ and a part of me wants to do _____," or "on the one hand, I feel _____ and on the other hand, I also feel _____." We might not realize what is happening, but these "parts" of us are just that; they are differing pieces of our psychological selves (in our brains) that get triggered or activated. One label that psychologists have given these parts is schema modes.

According to Jeffrey Young "a schema mode is: a facet of the self, involving specific schemas or coping responses that has not been fully integrated with other facets. According to this perspective, schema modes can be characterized by the degree to which a particular schema mode state has become dissociated, or cut off, from an individual's other modes. A schema mode, therefore, is a part of the self that is cut off, to some degree, from other aspects of the self."[16,]

"A schema mode, therefore, is a part of the self that is cut off, to some degree, from other aspects of the self."

The various modes have been organized into four categories. There are dysfunctional child modes, the dysfunctional parent modes, dysfunctional coping modes, and the healthy modes. The following are brief descriptions of each of these types of modes:

---

[16] "Schema Modes" accessed 5 September 2016, www.schematherapy.com/id61.htm

Dysfunctional Child Modes are associated with intense negative emotions such as rage, sadness, and abandonment. They are much like the concept of an "inner child" that is described in some psychotherapies.[17]

Dysfunctional Parent Modes is also a highly emotional mode, and it is conceptually similar to what Psychodynamic theory describes as introjects or representations of others that are psychologically taken inside a person. In this case, the dysfunctional parent responses to the child are taken-in or internalized. In the dysfunctional parent mode, for example, people keep putting pressure on themselves or hate themselves.

Dysfunctional Coping Modes are related to avoidant, surrendering, or over-compensating schema (core belief) coping in the person. People in an avoidant mode, avoid emotions and other inner experiences, or avoid social contact with others. When in an over-compensating coping mode, people stimulate or in some way inflate (aggrandize) their own importance in order to experience the opposite of their actual schema-related emotions.

Healthy Modes are those of healthy adults and happy children. In healthy adult modes, people are able to view life and their psychological selves in a realistic way. They are able to fulfill obligations, but at the same time can care for their own needs and well-being. This is similar to the psychodynamic concept of "healthy ego functioning." The happy child mode is related to fun, joy, and play.[18]

---

[17] It is interesting that the Apostle Paul, in 1 Corinthians 1:20, employs a similar idea with regard to how his readers were to think. They were to not be children in their thinking.

[18] Arntz and Jacob, *Schema Therapy in Practice: An Introductory Guide to the Schema Mode Approach*, 36-37.

Relevance of Modes for Life Coaching

What does this have to do with life coaching? Life coaches will experience their clients also shifting between their psychological parts or modes. For many people this shifting will be more like simply a change in mood, such as moving into a lonely mood or an angry mood. However, some clients will have stronger distinctions and differences between their modes, and these modes will not be as well connected to each other. The coach might react internally to the client's shift with a sense of, "Whoa, where did that come from?" or "Wow, I didn't see that coming!" or even, "Who is this person that just appeared?". It can also be difficult for life coaches to not have a spontaneous, unfiltered negative reaction to a client who has made a rather strong and possibly abrupt shift into a different mode.

Clients can be making good progress in the life coaching, but because of events between meetings, shift into a different mood or mode that they bring into the next meeting. This mode may not have surfaced before in the life coaching relationship. If the mode is more extreme and less connected to other modes, the life coaching process may be interrupted, because the person has shifted into a part of himself/herself that is less able to benefit from the coaching. The life coach needs to continue being relationally consistent, even though the client has shifted. This can be a challenge, because the client is not doing as well and maybe is even being difficult, or is making risky and unwise choices. If the client's mode is more extreme, counseling may be necessary.

Though the unhealthy modes can be quite powerful and disturbing, they are merely psychological. This is not to minimize the influence of modes, especially an uncontrolled influence, but to put modes into the proper perspective. Modes are not the person. Modes are in the brain's psychological functioning. Life coaches can help clients remember that their persons can make choices (using their determinate wills). In other words, their persons (souls/spirits) are capable of influencing these brain-based psychological modes.

It's additionally important to keep in mind that when clients are believers, their persons have been regenerated and are growing in virtues, they have been freed from the power of sin, and the Holy Spirit is available in them to strengthen their person to influence the brain's psychological modes.

Modes are not the person. Modes are in
the brain's psychological functioning.

BASIC 6: Helping with Brain Management

Detachment Steps for the Person of Influence Inside Myself

Our persons can influence our brain related reactions and beyond to the whole person. Jeffrey Schwartz has researched Obsessive Compulsive Disorder (OCD) and has written about how OCD can be self-treated by following four steps. He has generalized these steps to apply to other deceptive brain messages as well:

1. **Relabel** – Identify your deceptive brain messages and the uncomfortable sensations; call them what they really are.

2. **Reattribute** – Change your perception of the importance of the deceptive brain messages; say why these thoughts, urges, and impulses keep bothering you; they are *false brain* messages (It's not ME, it's just my BRAIN!).

3. **Refocus** – Direct your attention toward an activity or mental process that is wholesome and productive – even while the false and deceptive urges, thoughts, impulses, and sensations are still present and bothering you.

4. **Revalue** – Clearly see the thoughts, urges, and impulses for what they are, simply sensations caused by deceptive brain messages that are not true and that have little to no value (they are something to dismiss, not focus on).[19]

Life coaching is not directly addressing psychological problems, like OCD, but the steps Schwartz outlines can be adapted for use. The immaterial person is the one who makes the choices to manage the material brain's personal reactions and deceptive messages. Life coaches can encourage their clients to address these personal issues and reactions. For example, life coaches can

---

[19] Schwartz, *You Are Not Your Brain: The 4-Step Solution for Changing Bad Habits, Ending Unhealthy Thinking, and Taking Control of Your Life*, 90-91.

remind clients of these steps, and they (their persons) can then remind themselves (the whole person). The detachment steps can be further clarified for life coaching clients to include:

1. **In Relabeling** – That the dysfunctional and sinful reactions (malfunctions) are brain and body reactions and not who they are as persons (though affecting the whole person).

2. **In Reattributing** – That the dysfunctional and sinful reactions are malfunctions (deceptive brain messages) in the physical brain and body.

3. **In Refocusing** – By defining these malfunctions (deceptive brain messages) as distinct from their persons (though affecting the whole person) and by making healthy, virtue-based choices instead.

4. **In Revaluing** – These malfunctions as being inconsistent with their persons and inconsistent with life management and flourishing.

The immaterial person is the one who makes the choices to manage the material brain's personal reactions and deceptive messages.

The problematic issues or deceptive brain messages are not denied, but they are put in perspective by the person taking a position of detachment (distinctness of the person)/self-distancing (decentering). This position is not just an abstract idea, because the detachment position is backed-up with or grounded and strengthened by knowledge of the reality that the person is actually and structurally not the same as the brain and body. Therefore, the person is able to make choices that impact the brain and body. The regenerate person's potential for this efficacy is understood to be even greater by having been re-created – again because of being freed from the power of sin, and being strengthened by the Holy Spirit.[20]

The problematic issues or deceptive brain messages are not denied, but they are put in perspective by the person taking a position of detachment (distinctness of the person)/self-distancing (decentering).

---

[20] In 2 Corinthians 10:5, the Apostle Paul instructs his readers about taking every thought captive. This would seem to be a type of internal detachment of the person from thoughts in the brain. For Paul to make this type of comment, about an action performed, there is implied in it his belief that it was within their ability to do.

BASIC 7: Healthy Boundaries

Boundaries in Life Coaching Practice

A boundary is a border or limit. It may be the farthest limit or a marked area. In life coaching, as in counseling, the term "boundaries" is used to define the emotional and physical space that we place between oneself and others. Setting proper boundaries is important for our mental and spiritual health, as well as for appropriately assisting others by maintaining boundaries in helping.

Boundaries are learned in early relationships, especially in families. The extent to which a person automatically has appropriate emotional and physical boundaries, in relationships, is to a large extend explained by the boundary quality of those early relationships. As well, faulty boundary setting and maintaining has its origins in early relationships, combined with the remaining effects of falleness. An improving character/virtue development, along with an increasing understanding of and effectiveness in boundary setting, will not only help the life coach to personally function well, but also have a positive relationship impact on clients.

In life coaching, as in counseling, the term "boundaries" is used to define the emotional and physical space that we place between oneself and others.

Compassion is a virtue in the Christian life and very important for the life coaching relationship, as long as the compassion stays within emotional and physical boundaries. Compassion Fatigue (CF) refers to the taking-in or taking-on of another person's problems, as one's own to feel and to be responsible for. Helper compassion fatigue is also known as secondary traumatization or secondary post-traumatic stress disorder, which is equivalent to PTSD.[21]

Compassion Fatigue is a state of exhaustion and dysfunction – biologically, psychologically, and socially. A common theme, in the research, is that work that is focused on the relief of clients' emotional suffering typically results in the helper's absorption of information about human suffering, which is stressful. Individuals differ and some are more able to tolerate exposure to stressors without negative manifestations, while others are not.

Compassion Fatigue (CF) refers to the taking-in or taking-on of another person's problems, as one's own to feel and to be responsible for.

An explanation of differing abilities to manage the stress relates to the effectiveness in maintaining boundaries. Boundaries serve as a filtering system and are foundational to use in coping with the stress that comes with helping others. Also differences in the presence and use of coping techniques to handle stressors are related to the impact of compassion fatigue. Research indicates helper well-being contributes to avoidance of compassion fatigue symptoms. Religion and spirituality (as a personally meaningful experience) were found to have a positive correlation with immunity to stressful situations[22].

Other areas of boundary maintaining in life coaching have to do with competence, and confidentiality. **Competence** means limiting helping to the areas in which one has knowledge, training, and experience. In life coaching, this means that the trained life coach can provide a certain kind of help. The goals that a life coach sets with a client need to match the type of helping competence

---

[21]   Simpson and Starkey, *Secondary traumatic stress, compassion fatigue, and counselor spirituality: Implications for counselors working with trauma.*
[22]   Ibid.

of the life coach. Life coaches are assisting clients with managing personal issues by deepening their real-time relationship with God and by growing in related virtues. The boundary of competence or limit would, for example, stop before moving into practicing counseling with its related types of goals that extend more deeply into psychological functioning.

> The goals that a life coach sets with a client need to match the type of helping competence of the life coach.

Boundaries are a way of describing the decisions and actions that limit the use of personal information given to life coaches by the clients. This is the issue of **confidentiality**. Certain professions are mandated to keep client information confidential and not release the information without client consent or by legal requirement. Life coaches do not come under these laws, but nonetheless need to guard what client information is released to and whom. Clients need to be informed that their information, from the life coaching "practice" meetings, will be shared with the supervisor, for the purpose of the life coach's training.

Another issue related to life coaching and boundaries has to do with whether to do life coaching with someone with whom there could be a **physical attraction**. There may appear to be a simple answer: don't do it! However, that does not adequately take into consideration the level of vulnerability of either or both people in the coaching relationship. This would be a concern if, for example, either person is currently in a problematic romantic relationship that could leave the person vulnerable to the attention/even caring of a person with whom there could be an attraction. By contrast, a significant age difference between the life coach and the client would likely mean a lower risk of boundary crossing. However, a general rule of only doing life coaching with individuals with whom there is not the potential for sexual attraction would be the safest and probably wisest policy.

The setting and maintaining of boundaries in life coaching reflects the functioning and flourishing of the life coach. When boundaries are operating well in a person, then there is evidence of the virtue of self-control — an ability to stay within the limits of the particular situation, with a particular person with whom there is a certain type of relationship. A positive byproduct of knowing the boundaries is a greater sense of peace and confidence that comes from knowing how, how much, and in what manner to help.

A positive byproduct of knowing the boundaries is a greater sense of peace and confidence that comes from knowing how, how much, and in what manner to help.

BASIC 8: Life Coaching the Not-Consciously-Christian

Life coaching, as here defined, promotes a way of assisting others who consciously identify with and are committed to Christ. However, Christian workers value and find themselves forming relationships with people who are not so identified with Christ or who have not yet come to a point of consciously making a commitment to live their lives in relationship with Him.

The question arises of how to do life coaching when in a helping relationship with a person who is not identified with Christ. The life coaching material and approach seem so blatantly and intentionally Christian, and the life coaching goals appear so grounded in both persons (life coach and client) being consciously Christians[23].

Taking a Step Back

It is true that the life coaching approach is thoroughly integrated with a Christian view of the person and the person in relationship with God through Christ and empowered by the Holy Spirit. Although this is true, there are broader truths that can be illuminated and will provide for the latitude to apply life coaching to working with the not-consciously-Christian.

---

[23] I am intentionally using the terms "not-consciously-Christian or consciously Christian," but not to muddy the waters and imply that there is no "all-or-nothing" about being a Christian. There are two categories: saved (Christian or born-again believer) and unsaved (non-Christian or unbeliever). However, in doing evangelism in a Western European country, it becomes apparent that coming to Christ is both a point in time and experienced as a linear process. The point in time is when God acts to regenerate the person (the new birth from above). The person may not immediately become conscious that this has happened, so there may be a process over time of coming to an understanding – to become consciously Christian. Also, both those *who are not born-again* and those *who are, but are not-yet-fully-conscious-of-it*, are here described as being not-consciously-Christian. The life coach will have difficulty distinguishing between these two situations and will need to proceed similarly with people in both groups, because they are both not-consciously-Christian. Hence, there is a need for an adapted approach – one less overtly Christian.

An approach to this application of life coaching is to ask oneself what is common between Christians and non-Christians. Further, one can consider what concepts and principles in the life coaching material can be described or labeled more generally. This process will clarify both what is possible to retain from the original life coaching material and what is lost in this re-interpretation. The thoughts offered here are in the formative stage and continued consideration, application, and input will further clarify how to assist others who are not-consciously-Christian.

An approach to this application of life
coaching is to ask oneself what is common
between Christians and non-Christians.

What is Retained When Coaching the Not-Consciously-Christian?

The goals for life coaching can be retained, but in a modified form. Life coaching has **three primary life goals**. The **first** goal in life coaching is to strengthen the here and now (real-time) relationship the other person has with God. Obviously, the not-consciously-Christian are not going to have a Christian God concept. As will become apparent throughout the revisions for unbelievers, a concept of God has to be replaced with a concept of connecting to something transcendent. In Alcoholics Anonymous, references to God are replaced with the term "higher power."[24] In adapting life

---

[24] I think it would be quite difficult to use any twelve-step related material if the person is unable to accept and identify with some kind of personal higher power. A higher power to connect-with is a foundational twelve-step principle.

coaching for the not-consciously-Christian, using "higher power"[25] instead of God affords a way of retaining something that the client can connect with both as other-than-ones-self and as offering something for oneself. As well, attention can be paid to beliefs that the person has about relationships in general.

Secondly, life coaching encourages growth in character (virtue development). This goal and its accompanying concept can be easily retained. The idea of developing character through growth in personal virtues is not unique to Christianity. In the realm of helping relationships, the value of virtues has been illuminated and elevated in its significance in the past decade by the positive psychology movement. The development of virtues and character is an acceptable outcome in personal growth or self-improvement.

In life coaching, reaching these two aforementioned primary goals leads to accomplishing **a desired third goal**: improved personal coping and resilience. Life coaching, as describe in its explicitly Christian form, seeks to effectively assist in bringing about, through improved relating with God and increased character formation, enhanced personal functioning. The individual is thus enabled to better manage and transcend personal issues and challenges, as well as to make positive progress in life. The question arises about whether the same goal fits when life coaching those not-consciously-Christian, and it would seem that the answer is, "yes." Even those not in Christ are capable of improving with

---

[25] From a Christian perspective, we are very clear about who our higher power is (and we should disclose this to our clients), but from a more general perspective on a higher power it can be defined differently depending on the person. Here's a quote from the aaagostica website: "The Higher Power of the original 12 Steps is a spiritual idea. A Higher Power can be a God or another kind of symbol. It can be goodness, love, a friend or an idea. It can be our own intellectual curiosity. It can even be the 12-Step program itself. When we open ourselves to the power of spiritual resources, we open ourselves to an abundance of help that is beyond our comprehension. Each of us will find different powers, and those we use may change from day to day." http://aaagnostica.org/2014/03/26/step-2/ Accessed 5 September 2016

regard to increased coping and resilience in life. This improvement should not come as a surprise for two reasons that will be further examined in a later section: human nature and common grace.

What is Lost When Life Coaching the Not-Consciously-Christian?

What is the downside and what are the disadvantages to doing life coaching with the revised goals mentioned above? In other words, what is lost when taking out the references to a relationship with God, as He is known to Christians, and to the character formation process of becoming more Christ-like. Obviously, there is a world of difference and a huge loss in terms of the Gospel and salvation. This is not being minimized here or re-interpreted into some type of mere psychological or human improvement language.

The *first* goal is strengthening the here and now (real-time) relationship the other person has with God. Anything else, any other "higher power" is not really sufficiently powerful or personal. Yes, there is a form of transcendence that is built-into creation, both in the capacity of the person to reach out beyond herself and in, for example, the natural beauty of this world — a potential to connect to something more, but obviously this is limited. The relationship focus is also more limited to the life coach's modelling and encouraging of better relatedness with others.

With regard to the *second* goal, there is a limited opportunity for the not-consciously-Christian person to experience virtue formation. The types of virtues and their definitions will not necessarily conform exactly to those that are biblically informed. The life coach will need to navigate between his or her own perspective and the client's perspective. There cannot be a final appeal to the Bible for a corrective or authoritative reference regarding which virtues and how they are to be defined. However, there can be a mutual exploration of "virtues" in order to determine if a virtue is actually one that will provide the desired outcome. The loss here is one of clear direction. Without the Bible as a reference, there is no truly reliable moral compass. However practically speaking, most not-consciously-Christian clients will likely agree with the majority of virtues that are congruent with a Christian perspective. For the person who is not only not-consciously-Christian, but also not born-again, there are the additional limitations of not being freed from the power of sin and not having the empowering of the Holy Spirit for virtue formation.

The loss here is one of clear direction.
Without the Bible as a reference, there is no
truly reliable moral compass.

The **desired third goal** is an improved personal coping and resilience. Life coaching, as describe in its explicitly Christian form, seeks to effectively assist in bringing about, through improved relating with God and increased character formation, enhanced personal functioning. This same goal is appropriate for unbelievers as well. Unbelievers and others not-consciously-Christian are capable of these changes and improvements. The loss when working, especially with unbelievers, is one of potential. Both believers and unbelievers are capable of personal growth and change, including improved coping and resilience. The difference in potential, with more for believers, is because of being regenerated and because of the presence of the Holy Spirit — though this potential is not fully actualized in any particular believer. Potential here means how much is ultimately possible to be achieved. Therefore because we are talking about a potential and not what is actual for all, by comparison, at any given point in time some unbelievers will have made more progress than some believers with regard to enhanced functioning.

Human Nature Constants

The above clarifications regarding the goals in life coaching clients who are not-consciously-Christian are based on assumptions about human nature. One major assumption is that all people are both material and immaterial beings. In particular, all people have an immaterial soul. The unbeliever is also made in the image of God and as such retains a semblance of this unique image – e.g., uniquely human versus the rest of creation. Into this condition is also the experience of God's common grace in which God "sends rain on the just and the unjust." (Matthew 5:45b)

However, the striking difference (as alluded to previously) is that the believer's soul is regenerated (and justified in Christ) – made new in desires, freed from the power of sin, and strengthened by the Holy Spirit for sanctification. A believer is redeemed in soul, but still struggling with the not yet fully redeemed body. By contrast, though there is a soul within the unbeliever, it is not a redeemed soul. The unbeliever is in a state of being unredeemed both in soul and body. There is still potential for improvement in character, but again not as great a potential for growth as in the person who is born again and has the Holy Spirit. This unredeemed condition of an unbelieving client will likely become apparent while preceding with the client through the life coaching process. Though the difference between the believer and unbeliever is difficult to describe concretely, the term "lost" (as associated with those not yet saved) will make more sense experientially. There will likely be, in unbelievers, a less sharp distinction between the desires of the soul and the desires of the flesh, whereas in believers there can be a clearer distinction between godly desires of the soul and the sinful desires of the flesh.

In summary, the basic structure of human nature is the same for both those who are in-Christ and those not in Christ. As such, life coaching can also be used to assist unbelievers to have some measure of control over and influence on changing their whole persons. The life coaching work with people who are not-consciously-Christian is important. There is value in this helping in-and-of-itself, apart from any evangelistic potential. However, going through the process may actually become pre-evangelistic for some who will eventually come to Christ. The material provided here is not intended to in any way minimize the significance of or value of assisting others who are not-consciously-Christian, neither is it intended to devalue them as persons. It is a good thing to make life coaching available to all who have a need and are interested in this type of relationship.

A believer is redeemed in soul, but still
struggling with the not yet fully redeemed body.
By contrast, though there is a soul within
the unbeliever, it is not a redeemed soul.

BASIC 9: Putting It All Together

The following are ten points or tasks (previously listed in Basic 2) that are important to incorporate into the leading of life coach meetings. They are components that form an underlying structure to be used by life coaches. These points will first be listed, then some background information provided, and lastly the ten tasks will be further explained.

Ten Tasks: How to Lead a Life Coaching Meeting

1. Begin the meeting with, "What's most important for you to talk about today?"

2. Actively listen to the *story* (Basic 2) using the life coach *attitudes* (Basic 3).

3. Understand what clients want and set *situational goals* (Basic 2).

4. Find out what stands in the way of reaching the situational goals, such as shifting client *parts* or modes (see Basic 5).

5. Explore, with clients, for their *deepest desires* (person-centered godly and positive goals – Basic 2) related to the story.

6. Agree on practical *action* (Basic 2) steps to reach goals.

7. Identify the related *virtues* (see Basic 4) that need to be strengthened.

8. Provide an explanation about God's *here and now* involvement in their story or how their higher power can be of benefit.

9. Remind clients about using **detachment** (see Basic 6) – that their persons can manage their brains and bodies.

10. As needed, **teach** clients about and **model** for them the life coaching concepts and process, especially whenever they seem confused and unclear.

Background for The Ten Tasks

An underlying reality, for the life coach to continually keep in mind, is the perspective of the client being both an **immaterial person** and a **material brain and body**, yet also a whole person. The life coach understands that his immaterial person and the client's immaterial person are the conscious beings who are interacting in the life coaching meetings. Though each individual's material brain and body are involved, immaterial persons are animating them.

Whatever is happening in the meetings, in either the life coach or the client, is originating with these immaterial persons. This is significant especially for the client, because it means that what occurs in the brain and body of the client is at least potentially subject to the authority of the client's person. The brain and body of the client may exert a substantial force, but in normal functioning people, it is the person who has the actual agency (the capacity to act independently). The person of the client is who the life coach is addressing and encouraging to be engaged in the process of life coaching.

The Ten Tasks

Now, let's think about the ten tasks or components (listed above), in terms of their being resources for the life coach to draw upon and interventions to use while meeting with a client. Early in the meeting is the time when the life coach asks the client what's most important to the client to talk about or perhaps of most concern or most urgent to talk about in the meeting.

The life coach then invites the client to talk about this important personal topic or "story." As the client is disclosing her *story/* topic, that is her most important issue to talk about in the meeting, the life coach keeps the core conditions or *attitudes* in mind and practices them. So, on the side of the life coach, there is outwardly a relating with *Congruence*, *Positive Regard*, and *Empathy*. At the same time, the life coach is inwardly considering the client's story and possible goals.

The life coach needs to be listening to what is behind what the client is actually saying. The life coach would be "listening behind" for indications of:

1. The quality of person's here and now/*real-time relationship with God* or a *real-time use of a higher power*.

2. The type and strength of *virtues* that are involved or need to be involved.

3. Whether the client is shifting internally (in her brain) into differing *parts* or modes that are interfering (if dysfunctional) or assisting (if healthy).

> The life coach needs to be listening to what is behind what the client is actually saying.

The life coach would comment on these three areas as appropriate. The appropriate introduction to clients of information and encouragements concerning these areas is a skill for the life coach to develop over time and is enhanced through supervision.

Client and life coach references to the *quality of their relationship with God* and to *virtues* are connected with the first two *goals* in life coaching. The life coach has to exercise self-discipline to keep the focus inclusive of these two goals. Practical goals that will also emerge from the client's story are much more tangible and can easily become the main focus (e.g., a goal for a client to talk to the friend, with whom there was conflict, and to apologize and ask for forgiveness). **Relationship with God** goals (e.g., a client actively thinking about God's grace and kindness while going to the friend and talking to the friend) and strengthening *virtues* goals (e.g., a client being open to growing in humility and practicing humility when going to the friend and talking to the friend), are less tangible but no less real and are even more important than the practical and more behavioral goals.

Practical goals that will also emerge from the client's story are much more tangible and can easily become the main focus.

It is a challenge to be aware of and listen for indications of a client having shifted into a **dysfunctional mode** or part (e.g., a dysfunctional child mode). These modes are psychological processes functioning in the brain. Knowing that the dysfunctional modes occur and their characteristics, as well as having clarity about how clients would be responding when in them, prepares the life coach in a general way. It will likely require the help of a supervisor to initially assist in the identifying of a particular client's expression of modes. The dysfunctional modes are the problematic ones, but there are also **healthy modes** that life coaches need to recognize and that clients need to be encouraged toward using.

Life coaching is not about trying to change client modes, because that would be a goal for counseling or psychotherapy. Rather, the life coach identifies the mode, helps clients understand when it's happening, and lends support to the client's person. This support is in the form of helping to improve the client's **real-time relationship with God** and growth in the client's **virtues**, so that both are strengthened for use when a mode is triggered. Therefore, the person will be more able to make positive choices that are also healthy and godly.

The lending of this type of life coach support is not only for managing modes, but is also for every personal issue and situation that the client is experiencing. As well, the support from the life coach will need to include reminders to the client that the modes, as well as the other personal internal struggles and issues are happening in their brains. The life coach can further this support by reminding the client about the **detachment steps** that help a person self-distance from these personal issues and, again, make positive choices.

The life coaching **relationship** is the context for all this life coach support and assistance to clients. When the life coach is relating with the **attitudes/core conditions**, then the relationship path between him and the client is created and open for modeling **virtues** that the client can internalize. The positive effect of this virtues-modeled-in-a-healthy-relationship by the life coach can be heard in client comments such as, "When the problem was happening, I remembered what you would say to me and how you would relate to me, and then I did the same."

Additional Comments on the Ten Tasks

These ten tasks are the primary life coaching components that are intentionally introduced into the life coaching meetings. The ten tasks will normally occur in each meeting, but not always. For example, the client shifting into dysfunctional modes may not happen in every meeting.

> When the life coach is relating with the attitudes/ core conditions, then the relationship path between him and the client is created and open for modeling virtues that the client can internalize.

Doing life coaching can be the primary reason for the relationship, but it can also be used as an add-on or adjunctive way to assist, when meetings have been happening for other purposes (e.g., the relationship started with a bible study or as discipleship focus, or possibly to be a supportive person). Life coaching would typically be added to the relationship when there are personal issues that come up, and that are interfering and of concern. Life coaching would be combined with this other focus for the relationship by taking a break in the original focus for a while in order to have a life coaching concentration on personal issues. Or, life coaching could be integrated into the meetings and be done concurrently with the original focus (e.g., doing a bible study while keeping the personal issues in mind).

These ten tasks are obviously not covering everything. Life coaching has a narrow and specific purpose reflected in its three goals; having as the desired end state an improved personal coping and resilience, inclusive of a deeper real-time relationship with God or use of a higher power and strengthened character. Life coaching does not have all the answers, and it is not designed to replace other ways to foster growth and healing. It is not being promoted as the only way to grow personally and spiritually. The life coaching approach is simply a tool to help, in a specific way, to get through personal difficulties and have improved personal stability.

Once life coaches learn how to use the ten tasks, they can add to it what they believe to be of additional importance. Exercises that improve self-distancing could be beneficial. For those consciously Christian this could also include, for example, incorporating specific spiritual disciplines to deepen real-time relating with God and growth in character virtues.

BASIC 10: The Motivation and Means to Change

The Motivation to Change

If we want to understand why people change (that is, why they make internal personal changes), we have to consider the issue of motivation. From my experience practicing as a clinical psychologist, I'd have to say that most of the time we really don't want to change, or at least we don't want to change as deeply as it is needed. In other words, to be motivated to change usually takes something intensely negative happening internally (e.g., a panic attack) and/ or a push from outside our selves (e.g., a crisis). This is where the "life" in life coaching begins to make more sense. Life provides ample motivation in the form of challenges and suffering. I know that we sometimes embrace personal growth, but that is for a pleasant, cosmetic sort of change. However, life puts us under-the-knife, so to speak, of real and potentially deeper level change.

I'd have to say that most of the time we really don't want to change, or at least we don't want to change as deeply as it is needed.

The change mentioned above is not to be confused with the motivation that people have to be better in some manner. Particular individuals may not appear to have this motivation or the motivation might be turned in a destructive or negative direction, but it is still there. There seems to be this, possibly innate tendency in humans toward bettering themselves in some way.

Christians share this desire, but it is altered in their person as a desire to become more like Christ – to grow in the virtuous character of Christ that was implanted in their persons at regeneration. In this sense, Christians have an additional motivation or perhaps a clarified goal for their motivation, even while their unredeemed brains and bodies put up barriers (personal dysfunctions and sinful desires) to this motivation.

So, even though people share a common desire to be better and work toward progress, making internal personal changes is different. This type of change requires being motivated, as by a strong external or internal negative event.

The Means to Change

Human challenges and suffering are, from a secular worldview, random. In other words, though one can pursue the finding meaning from the events after they happen, there is no purposefulness behind them. There is no one directing the events — no one with the intent and power to bring about a particular goal.

This is not the perspective of those who believe in an all-powerful God. Events are seen as providential — under the authority of a God who has the power to bring about his purposes. Christians believe in all-powerful God who is also all-good. Not only does God bring meaning in and from the events of life, but also He pre-determines the events to bring about His good purposes that He is able to fulfill, even if humans are not aware of what He is doing.

From what has just been said about God's providence, we can derive that behind our change is the "hand of God." However, this is not to say that He has left us out of the process of change. People, it seems, often want magic and not hard, consistent work to bring about personal change. For Christians, this desire for magic might seem like a faithful reliance on a supernatural God. In some measure that is likely often the case. However, there is the matter of personal responsibility. What God can do and how God usually does act needs to be considered. Even though God is able to supernaturally bring about change, He routinely combines His working with ordinary means and human effort (e.g., spiritual disciplines and psychological interventions).

> People, it seems, often want magic and not hard,
> consistent work to bring about personal change.

A continued wishing for a magical change, especially when God clearly is not answering, may be an unwillingness for persons to take responsibility for changing and being open to using the ordinary means. In other words, behind the appeals for God to work miraculously just might be a resistance to change. Again, life challenges and suffering not only are a motivation to seek change and take responsibility for it, but also might be a way to get persons be to open to using the ordinary means God has allowed humans to discover. Of course, this is not an either/or choice, but rather a both/and situation. The person is cooperatively putting effort into change, while God is also at work.

Life coaching promotes the idea that change is best when it is coming from motivated responsibility and cooperation. In other words, the person is ready and willing to change, believes change is possible by his/her efforts, is open to using the means provided, and additionally if regenerated, practices faithful reliance on God purposefully bringing about His good. The "life" in life coaching is also intended to mean that people who have been helped through an issue or challenge by a life coach, need to keep applying to their lives the components that have been learned. By doing so, they will be responsibly cooperating with means to strengthen coping and resilience. For Christians, this will specifically mean a continuing pursuit of a deepening here-and-now relationship with God and growing in Christ-like virtuous character.

Motivation and means can become more intrinsic. That is to say, when people begin to experience the positive benefits of change, then the push to change becomes more internal. My hope is that life coaching will play a significant role in change happening in the present client circumstance and that there will be an increased internal commitment in clients to a life of continual positive change. As a life coach, you are coaching others in learning the means to responsibly manage their own lives in a healthy and godly manner.

References

Arntz, Arnoud and Gitta Jacob. *Schema Therapy In Practice: An Introductory Guide to the Schema Mode Approach.* Chichester, UK: Wiley —Blackwell, 2013

Egan, Gerard. *The skilled helper: A Problem-Management and Opportunity-Development Approach to Helping* (8th ed.). Pacific Grove, CA: Brooks/Cole Publishing, 2007

Frankl, Viktor. *The Unconscious God.* New York: Simon and Schuster, 1975.

Kirschenbaum, H. & Jourdan, A. "The Current Status of Carl Rogers and The Person-Centered Approach". *Psychotherapy: Theory, Research, Practice, Training.* 42 (1) (2005), 37-51.

McLeod, Saul. "Person Centered Therapy". *Simply Psychology. org*, 2015. www.simplypsychology.org/client- centred-therapy.html.

Morgan, Dennis. *An Introduction to Life Mentor Training.* Vienna, Austria (unpublished training material).

Morgan, Dennis. *The Soul That Suffers: A Perspective on Human Nature and Suffering for Counseling Christians.* Chesapeake, VA: Watertree Press, 2013.

Schwartz, Jeffery and Madden, Rebecca. *You Are Not Your Brain: The 4-Step Solution for Changing Bad Habits, Ending Unhealthy Thinking, and Taking Control of Your Life.* New York: Avery: 2011

Simpson, Laura R. and Starkey, Donna S. "Secondary Traumatic Stress, Compassion Fatigue And Counselor Spirituality: Implications For Counselors Working With Trauma". *Counselingoutfitters. com*, 2006. http://counselingoutfitters.com/Simpson.htm.

References

Appendix A: Human Nature Related Definitions, Locations, and Implications

Life coaching involves assisting persons in reaching spiritual goals in order to also better manage their lives. This is a work that is closely connected to human nature (anthropology). As such, it requires that there be a diligent attempt to understand the nature of the human person. Life coaching approaches the coaching relationship from a biblical world-view perspective. Therefore, the understanding of human nature, in life coaching, must be biblically informed and consistent with biblical teaching.

When considering a biblical view of human nature, a biblical anthropology, two key points of reference should be prominent: creation and re-creation. In creation, according to the biblical account, humans were created as composed of two substances: body and soul (i.e., material and immaterial). This needs to be thoroughly understood in order to understand human nature. The fact that mankind was created in the image of God includes this dualistic composition (actually a dualism and yet whole persons – a holistic dualism).

In re-creation, the new birth, there is a setting right what went wrong after creation, in the Fall. This re-creation is what it means to be born again – the term: regeneration. Regeneration is a unilateral act of God, on the human soul, that begins the order of salvation (the ordo-salutis). Though all mankind is in the image of God, only those that God calls have their souls re-created (are given a new "heart"). This regeneration too is highly critical and must also be thoroughly understood for its human nature implications.

These two points (creation and re-creation) are the starting points for understanding human nature. Since the Bible is not intended to be or organized to systematically reveal an anthropology, careful research and thought must be given to determining what the Bible says about human nature, while also considering the implications of the developed view of human nature. The following definitions, locations, and implications are important points for constructing an anthropology that accurately represents biblical teaching and considers the need to make a clear representation of that anthropology so as to be useful in life coaching. Please consider the following points as a work in progress, not as a mere speculation, but as an honest and rational, yet limited attempt to remain faithful to Scripture and open to further clarifications.

Definitions

Defining Humans as Having Two Substances

Human beings are composed of two substances: immaterial and material. The immaterial substance is referred to as the soul or spirit. The material substance is the brain and body. In the earthly existence there are these two parts housed within one whole person, and there is interaction and influencing between the two.

Defining Humans as Only Having One Nature

Human beings can only have one nature. The only exception to this is Jesus. He being God, took on a human body and human nature. In this incarnation, he had both his nature as God and a human nature – fully God and fully man. Mankind can only have one nature that is either the old sinful nature or the new regenerate nature. Having been given a new or recreated nature in regeneration, however, does not eliminate all the effects of having been fallen. Sinful dispositions remain.

Defining the Person as the Soul/Spirit

The person, sometimes referred to biblically as the innermost being, is the soul or spirit of the whole person. This can simply be identified as who one is referring to when saying "I". The person is not to be confused with psychological and other brain related processes. The person is conscious and wills the whole person, through the animating of the brain and body.

> Mankind can only have one nature that is either
> the old sinful nature or the new regenerate nature.

Defining Regeneration

A strong view of regeneration affirms that God has to initiate salvation and his first work is to recreate the soul/spirit of the whole person. This is a new birth for the soul/spirit and both frees the person from the power of sin and makes the soul already perfect in Christ, ready for growth in Christ-likeness that then influences the material part of the person, through the empowering of the Holy Spirit.

Locations

Locating the Person in the Soul/spirit

The location of the immaterial person is made more difficult by virtue of the fact that what is immaterial does not occupy physical space. Defining the person as the soul/spirit, however, does not change the fact that the location of the person (the immaterial substance) is in the whole person. Being part of the whole person, this immaterial part exists in some connection with the material part of the whole person, while in the earthly existence. However, this connection does not mean that the soul is located in a particular place in the body or that a loss of some body part would change the soul. For example, the soul is not located in the body such that if a leg is removed from the body, then a portion of the soul has been lost as well. Additionally, the soul is capable of a continued existence apart from the body (i.e., in the intermediate state after physical death.)

Defining the person as the soul/spirit, however, does
not change the fact that the location of the person
(the immaterial substance) is in the whole person.

Locating the Nature of the Person

The one nature of the whole person is either old (unregenerate in
the unbeliever) or new (regenerate in the believer). One way to
determine where the nature is located is to consider what is the
case for a believer, who has a new nature and has been restored to
a relationship with God. The location of the new nature would not
be in the body, since the body has not yet been redeemed in the
believer. The new nature is located in the person who is embodied
in the whole person. The person's nature influences the brain/
body and can have dominance over the remaining sinful desires in
the brain/body, the flesh (in the negative sinful sense). The new
nature is the nature of the regenerate person (immaterial soul/
spirit), that has been renewed and is growing in Christ-likeness.

Locating Regeneration

Christians have had their person (soul/spirit) supernaturally
made new. Even with this regeneration, the person is still located
within the whole person (with it's material part – the brain and
body). Redemption has already been completed by Christ, but
is not yet fully experienced in this life. The regeneration effect,
in this life on earth, is located in the person (soul/spirit), and
the person is located in the whole person. Until death, there is
a work of sanctification taking place in the whole person (soul/
spirit growing in character and affecting the brain and body to
transform its sinful desires and actions, by the empowering of
the Holy Spirit). After death, the regenerate person awaits the
promised new body that will be given at the final resurrection, and
regeneration will extend throughout the whole person.

Locating the Fruit of the Spirit

The fruit of the Spirit is a product of the believer's person (regenerated immaterial soul/spirit) and the working of the Holy Spirit. Though the source of the fruit is the person (immaterial) empowered by the Holy Spirit, the fruit flows through the rest of the whole person — through the material brain and body.

Locating the Flesh

The flesh (sinful nature) is extensive in the unbeliever (i.e., it extends to the whole person of the unbeliever — both immaterial and material). The whole person of the unbeliever remains under the power of sin, and though unbelievers are capable of producing what are externally good works, because of common grace and being in the image of God, these good works do not come from a heart made new and clean (the new nature). The location of the flesh in believers cannot be the same as unbelievers, because of regeneration. The person (soul/spirit) has been born again and given a new nature that is no longer corrupt. This does not mean that the whole person is no longer corrupt. The believer, as a whole person is a combination of a redeemed person and not yet redeemed body (material substance). The flesh refers to the continued location and existence, in this life, of sinful dispositions in the brain/body of the believer.

Implications

Mapping of the Contours within the Whole Person

Life coaching provides a more tangible and organized mapping of human nature. By more clearly defining and locating the person as the soul/spirit, people can more readily differentiate and distinguish their person from the processes within the brain. Sin and personal issues can then be viewed from the perspective of not being the deepest desires of the person, but rather the functioning of the brain/body. With the inner sense of detachment from brain/body problematic functioning, the person can then more readily and effectively address these problems of sin and dysfunction. This mapping of the human nature of the whole person relies on biblically-based theological truth, especially regarding the supernatural and permanent change occurring in regeneration.

The flesh refers to the continued location
and existence, in this life, of sinful
dispositions in the brain/body of the believer.

Providing a more Solid foundation for Hope

When human nature is poorly understood as a muddled, mixture of internal processes, it is difficult for people to get a clear sense of their person apart from contaminated inner processes. When a person is in Christ, this confusion inhibits both a sense of being solidly new in Christ and being perfectly prepared to make progress in life. The effects of regeneration, justification, and sanctification should be understood as providing a solid new person who is enabled by the Holy Spirit to influence the brain and body, thus directing the whole person to being more consistently Christ-like. Seeing oneself in this manner both grounds and increases hope – a hope that one can experience change and in fact will be changed.

Allowing for Choice

The perhaps unintentional consequence of an unclear view of the person versus the brain and body, is to put limitations on the perceived ability to choose. Granted that unbelievers have not been freed from the power of sin, but even so, when unbelievers are able to affirm having an immaterial person they are enabled to identify more readily with an ability to make choices over internal processes and external behaviors of the material part. Believers, having a clear understanding that their persons are distinct from their brain and body functioning, are enabled potentially to an even greater extent to enact the choices that can be made, because of also being freed from the power of sin and empowered by the Holy Spirit.

The perhaps unintentional consequence
of an unclear view of the person versus the
brain and body, is to put limitations
on the perceived ability to choose.

Greater Sense of Renewal and Salvation

When a person in Christ does not have a well-defined understanding of the extent of the actual supernatural change in regeneration, then the sense of the renewal in salvation is distorted and minimized. With a well-defined and located understanding of human nature, along with a strong view of regeneration, there is an opportunity to more clearly contrast the already new person with the yet to be renewed brain and body. With an enhanced distinction between what is new (soul/spirit) and what is old (brain/body) in the whole person, there can be a greater sense of and confidence in the extent of salvation renewal that has occurred.

Biblical and theological teachings about salvation in Christ can have a ring of abstracted truth that is intellectually acknowledged, but not necessarily personally absorbed. When the internal contours within are clarified to distinguish the inner structure of the human being, then salvation can be identified as change that is specifically defined and located. Believers can recognize more fully and have a deeper grasp of the work accomplished in salvation — that salvation is a personal change already done in a definite part of oneself, even while still being in process in another definite part of oneself.

More Honesty that Comes from Assurance and Detachment

Hiding imperfect aspects of oneself and behavior from others is a self-protective attempt to keep from being unacceptable to another. This is a form of dishonestly, coming from fear. Hiding from God occurred in the Garden of Eden after disobedience. This hiding is not unlike what people commonly do in relationships. However, if one knows intellectually and personally that there is unconditional acceptance, then there is freedom from the fear of being unacceptable. A strong basis for the courage to be honest can be derived from the assurance of being a fully redeemed and accepted person in Christ, even while still having imperfections in the performance of the brain and body. The identity as a child of God then brings with it an assurance of acceptableness and a willingness to be more honest in the self-assessment of ongoing sinfulness and weakness. Because one can more honestly reveal imperfections when one is secure about being accepted by the other, communication can be more open. With this greater personal awareness and assurance of acceptance, admission of imperfections and confession of the shortcomings can be made more freely, and there can be a fuller cooperation with others toward personal and spiritual growth. This is the case in one's relationship with God as well, where the varied internal sanctification issues can be more extensively and fully addressed.

Clearer Perspective on the Internal Struggle

How can one really know the struggle between the fruit of the Spirit and the works of the flesh, when there is confusion about what parts of oneself are engaged in the conflict? If the person can internally step his/her person back from the fray and view the place where the battle is raging, then there is a valuable perspective from which to move forward. "I can do all things through Him who strengthens me." (Philippians 4:13). There is a "me" who He will strengthen, and a "we" who will together fight the battle. The believer's battle is understood to be between the person (soul/spirit) and the flesh (in the brain and body), with the person being empowered the Holy Spirit. The believer does not approach the struggle victoriously by saying "I am the badness I seek to defeat." Rather, the believer approaches the struggle by acknowledging that, "I am the new person enabled to defeat the non-person remaining imperfections."

No denial of Sin and the Impossibility of Perfection in this Life

It is a faulty conclusion to believe that because of the view expressed here of the soul already being perfect in Christ, that what is also being put forth is that Christians don't sin. That is a faulty conclusion because it misses the reality that in this life human beings are whole persons — the soul/spirit embedded in the whole person, together with the yet unredeemed body. Therefore, because of remaining sinful dispositions in the flesh, Christians do continue to sin in this life. The sinning is not because of a continued identity as a sinner (someone outside of an adopted relationship with God through Christ), but because of being a saint who still sins. God has adopted Christians, but their redemption though already accomplished and currently fulfilled in the soul/spirit, is not yet fulfilled in the body. Their body dies and has to undergo a resurrection/transformation.

The believer approaches the struggle by acknowledging that, "I am the new person enabled to defeat the non-person remaining imperfections."

Location and Reality of Psychological Processes and Problems

As stated previously, the view put forth here is that humans have a material part (the brain and the rest of the body) and an immaterial part (the soul or spirit) to their whole person, and the soul or spirit is the person. Remaining fallenness is understood to reside in the material part, i.e., in the brain and body. This could be misunderstood as saying that since sin has been eradicated, in the person (soul/spirit) by regeneration, then all that remains to be done can be accomplished through psychotherapy – the solution needed for repairing the problems remaining in the brain and body. This faulty conclusion may come from a difficulty understanding that there is still a sin problem – validating that even though the soul is already redeemed by regeneration, there is still a need for forgiveness and growth toward Christ-likeness.

There may also be a confusion of what it means to have sin, with what it means to have psychological problems. Psychological problems and their associated psychological processes are also a result of the Fall and are dysfunctions of the brain. These psychological issues and problems (psychopathology) are intangible. They are intangible, but no less real than the dysfunction that comes from a brain disorder like Dementia, Alzheimer's, or Schizophrenia.

Sin and psychopathology are two distinct but related conditions (both happening in the physical part of the person) that can impact each other. Not all sin is psychopathology and not all psychopathology is sin, just as not all thoughts and actions of the brain and body are sinful. The body was originally part of God's good creation. Of course, the Fall happened and every imperfection in humankind is a result of this Fall, so it can be said there is no good thing in the whole person. In this sense of separation from God in the Fall, there is nothing good that could be done in the body apart from the redemption in Christ Jesus. This principle is one category of sin – that coming from the Fall. It is of a different category than the category of sinful behaviors. The Bible indicates a distinguishing of sin as a principle that taints everything in creation, from sinful behaviors done in the body, and there is a Biblical recognition of both sinful and good behaviors that can be done in the body.

Not all sin is psychopathology and not all
psychopathology is sin, just as not all thoughts
and actions of the brain and body are sinful.

Locating the psychological problems in the material brain and body
is an important perspective for efficacy both spiritually and
psychologically. Personal efficacy means that the person's beliefs and
actions, about oneself and resources, are indicating having confidence
in the ability to change oneself. There is more empowerment of
efficacy when it is understood that one's person is distinct from one's
brain and body, and the person can make choices to effect change in
the brain and body. Further empowerment for efficacy occurs when
believers understand that not only is their person distinct from their
brain and body, but that their person has been freed from the power
of sin and the Holy Spirit strengthens their person.

Concluding Remarks

There are differing views about what happens in the person and
where it happens in the person with regard to regeneration. The
view presented here is that there is real supernatural recreation
of the soul (the new nature) and that the sinful desires of the old
nature still linger in the brain and body (the flesh), but Christians
indeed only have one nature – the new nature. Making this clear
distinct between soul and body is biblically supported and very
helpful for understanding the human role in the process of change,
especially Christians changing. By believing in this distinction, it
clarifies that one's impact on change (toward more Christ-likeness)
can be more effective and one's management of psychological
processes more possible. The life coaching perspective has a
real benefit for providing a solid spiritually-based equipping for
Christian workers to be ready to positively assist with the personal
issues that emerge in the people with whom they are ministering.

Some might question the wisdom and necessity of introducing into life coaching teachings views that could be considered different from common Christian thinking (i.e., a common Christian thinking that is often underdeveloped regarding a biblical view of human nature and related concepts). However, if the aforementioned definitions and locations were not included in life coaching, it could be asked, "What new insight or additional contribution does life coaching make?" The goals of deepening the here-and-now relationship with God and growth in Christ-like virtues are common-fair in assisting others from a Christian perspective. It is the third goal that would be seriously impoverished without the more developed and biblically grounded life coaching teaching on human nature. To effect change to personal resilience and the management of personal problems, requires a model of the structure and functioning of human nature that is both sound and beyond the commonplace.

The above explanations are provided because there might be questions about where the life coaching material is coming from both theologically and psychologically. Diligent effort has been put into developing life coaching from a clarified biblical view of human nature, so that it can accomplish more; so that through the life coaching relationship there can be a modification in one's ability to cope with personal issues and an experiencing of gains in resiliency. With a robust and accurate perspective and model of human nature and of assisting others with growth in relationship with God and in Christ-like character, there ought to be these significant implications of enhanced positive psychological functioning and personal resilience.

Appendix B: Life Goals and Situational Goals Together

This material is being presented to resolve possible confusion between the three broad and foundational goals of life coaching, the *life goals* and the goals of the stages of change, the *situational goals*. The three *life goals* are: 1. Strengthening the here-and-now (real-time) relationship with God or use of the higher power; 2. Growth in character (virtue development); and 3. Improved personal coping and resilience. The *situational goals* are related to the client's story and are individualized. In other words, the situational goals are client specific, depending on what needs to change for the client and what the client desires for a positive outcome.

These two sets of goals are being clarified and worked-on at the same time during the life coaching process. The *life goals* are general and are about important and foundational areas of growth for the client in order to have a more godly and/or healthy resilience in life. In a sense, they are also the foundational solution to the situational needs of the client. The *situational goals* are better resolved when progress has also being made in the life goals.

> The situational goals are better resolved when progress has also being made in the life goals.

That is to say, while taking action toward changing in some practical part of the client's life, the client is becoming more able to rely on her relationship with God (or use of a higher power) and is also practicing and growing in virtues that are needed to take action. For example, if the client has offended a friend and there has been conflict, the client needs to take action to repair the relationship – to apologize and ask for the friend's forgiveness. This will be done with more confidence if the she is trusting in God's active participation with her in the restoration with her friend. As well, if she is entering into the process of restoration with more self-awareness, humility, and patience, she will be communicating more clearly, congruently, and appropriately her desire for a restored relationship. The client would be taking actions that are simultaneously flowing out of both *situational* and *life goals* that are being blended and worked-on together.

BOOK 2:
An Introduction to Life Mentor Training

Introduction

Life Mentor Training

Life mentoring is a real helping relationship. It is not counseling or psychotherapy, even though there is a similar reason for deciding to help: a situation is causing a personal struggle in the other individual. Due to the other's personal issues and suffering, there is not only a need to assist the person to be able to cope better, but also to prevent the issues from interfering with making positive progress personally and spiritually.

Life mentoring has *three primary life goals*. The first two are easily understood and affirmed. *First*, life mentoring works to strengthen the here and now (real-time) relationship the other person has with God.[1] *Secondly*, life mentoring encourages growth in character (virtue development). However, reaching these two primary goals leads to accomplishing *a desired third goal*: improved personal coping and resilience. In other words, life mentoring seeks to effectively assist in bringing about, through improved relating with God and increased character formation, enhanced personal functioning. The individual is thus enabled to better manage and transcend personal life issues and challenges.

To accomplish these goals, life mentors help clients move through *three stages of change*.[2] The first stage is *Telling Their Story*. The second stage is *Setting Situational Goals*. The final stage is *Taking Action*. The character-based quality of the relationship between the life mentor and the client is the powerful context for change.

---

[1]   Life mentoring is offered both for people who consciously identify themselves as Christian and also for those who do not identify as consciously Christian (see Appendix A for information regarding life mentoring those who are not-consciously Christian). The goals are similar for both, with a distinction in the first goal: *First*, life mentoring works to strengthen the here and now (real-time) relationship the other person has with God or with reference to a higher power.

[2]   Egan, *The skilled helper: A Problem-Management and Opportunity-Development Approach to Helping*.

Life Mentor Training provides an opportunity for people to prepare to be life mentors by learning about and practicing the process of change that is associated with life mentoring. The training has three parts: a Pre-Class reading assignment, an Information Class, and the Practice Preparation that has two levels:

- The **Pre-Class** is the time prior to the in-class times, when participants are assigned to read *An Introduction to Life Mentor Training* and become familiar with the material in the book *Life in Process*.

- The **Information Class** is a one-day Life Mentor in-class training seminar covering the material in *An Introduction to Life Mentor Training* and is preparation for the post-class practice.

- **Practice Preparation** involves doing structured life mentoring as guided by the use of *Life in Process* worksheets and receiving supervision.

  - **Level I** preparation is held in a second day of in-class training — the **Partner Practice** — focused on practicing with a partner who is also a life mentor-in-training. During this in-class time, worksheets will be processed with the partner. Small group discussion times will also be used to clarify the mentoring process. In-class supervision and practice facilitation is provided.

  - **Level II** has the additional requirement that life mentors-in-training have a client that they are taking through the worksheets, while regularly attending supervision meetings to discuss the life mentoring practice experience — **Supervised Practice**.

Clarifying Human Nature Related Definitions, Locations, and Implications

Life mentoring involves assisting persons in reaching spiritual goals in order to also better manage their lives. This is a work that is closely connected to human nature (anthropology). As such, it requires that there be a diligent attempt to understand the nature of the human person. Life mentoring approaches the mentoring relationship from a biblical world-view perspective. Therefore, the understanding of human nature, in life mentoring, must be biblically informed and consistent with biblical teaching.

When considering a biblical view of human nature, a biblical anthropology, two key points of reference should be prominent: creation and re-creation. In creation, according to the biblical account, humans were created as composed of two substances: body and soul (i.e., material and immaterial). This needs to be thoroughly understood in order to understand human nature. The fact that mankind was created in the image of God includes this dualistic composition (actually a dualism and yet whole persons − a holistic dualism).

In re-creation, the new birth, there is a setting right what went wrong after creation, in the Fall. This re-creation is what it means to be born again − the term: regeneration. Regeneration is a unilateral act of God, on the human soul, that begins the order of salvation (the ordo-salutis). Though all mankind is in the image of God, only those that God calls have their souls re-created (are given a new "heart"). This regeneration too is highly critical and must also be thoroughly understood for its human nature implications.

These two points (creation and re-creation) are the starting points for understanding human nature. Since the Bible is not intended to be or organized to systematically reveal an anthropology, careful research and thought must be given in determining what the Bible says about human nature, while also considering the implications of the developed view of human nature. The following definitions, locations, and implications are important points for constructing an anthropology that accurately represents biblical teaching and considers the need to make a clear representation of that anthropology so as to be useful in life mentoring. Please consider the following points as a work in progress, not as a mere speculation, but as an honest and rational, yet limited attempt to remain faithful to Scripture and is open to further clarifications.

Human Nature Related Definitions

Defining Humans as Having Two Substances

Human beings are composed of two substances: immaterial and material. The immaterial substance is referred to as the soul or spirit. The material substance is the brain and body. In the earthly existence these two substances are housed within one whole person, and there is interaction and influencing between the two.

Defining Humans as Only Having One Nature

Human beings can only have one nature. The only exception to this is Jesus. He being God, took on a human body and human nature. In this incarnation, he had both his nature as God and a human nature – fully God and fully man. Mankind can only have one nature that is either the old sinful nature or the new regenerate nature. Having been given a new or recreated nature in regeneration, however, does not eliminate all the effects of having been fallen. Sinful dispositions remain.

Defining the Person as the Soul/Spirit

The person, sometimes referred to biblically as the innermost being, is the soul or spirit of the whole person. This can simply be identified as who one is referring to when saying "I." The person is not to be confused with psychological and other brain related processes. The person is conscious and wills the whole person, through the animating of the brain and body.

Defining Regeneration

A strong view of regeneration affirms that God has to initiate salvation, and His first work, within the individual, is to recreate the person (soul/spirit) of the whole person. This is a new birth for the soul/spirit that makes the person free from the power of sin and in this part, of the whole person, already perfect in Christ. The person (soul/spirit) then influences the material part of his/her whole person, through the empowering of the Holy Spirit, toward growth in Christlikeness.

Human Nature Related Locations

Locating the Person in the Soul/spirit

The location of the immaterial person is made more difficult in virtue of the fact that what is immaterial does not occupy physical space. Defining the person as the soul/spirit, however, does not change the fact that the location of the person (the immaterial substance) is in the whole person. Being part of the whole person, this immaterial part exists in some connection with the material part of the whole person, while in the earthly existence. However, this connection does not mean that the soul is located in a particular place in the body or that a loss of some body part would change the soul. For example, the soul is not located in the body such that if a leg is removed from the body, then a portion of the soul has been lost as well. Additionally, the soul is capable of a continued existence apart from the body (i.e., in the intermediate state after physical death.)

Locating the Nature of the Person

The one nature of the whole person is either old (unregenerate in the unbeliever) or new (regenerate in the believer). One way to determine where the nature is located is to consider what the case is for a believer, who has a new nature and has been restored to a relationship with God. The location of the new nature would not be in the body, since the body has not yet been redeemed in the believer. The new nature is located in the person who is embodied in the whole person. The person's nature influences the brain/body and can have dominance over the remaining sinful desires in the brain/body, the flesh (in the negative sinful sense). The new nature is the nature of the regenerate person (immaterial soul/spirit), that has been renewed and is growing in Christ-likeness.

Locating Regeneration

Christians have had their person (soul/spirit) supernaturally made new. Even with this regeneration, the person is still located within the whole person (with its material part — the brain and body). Redemption has already been completed by Christ, but is not yet fully experienced in this life. The regeneration effect, in this life on earth, is located in the person (soul/spirit), and the person is located in the whole person. Until death, there is a work of sanctification taking place in the whole person (soul/spirit growing in character and affecting the brain and body to transform its sinful desires and actions, by the empowering of the Holy Spirit). After death, the regenerate person awaits the promised new body that will be given at the final resurrection, and regeneration will extend throughout the whole person.

Locating the Fruit of the Spirit

The fruit of the Spirit is a production of the believer's person (regenerated immaterial soul/spirit) and the working of the Holy Spirit. Though the source of the fruit is the person (immaterial) empowered by the Holy Spirit, the fruit flows through the rest of the whole person — through the material brain and body.

Locating the Flesh

The flesh (sinful nature) is extensive in the unbeliever (i.e., it extends to the whole person of the unbeliever — both immaterial and material). The whole person of the unbeliever remains under the power of sin, and though unbelievers are capable of producing what are externally good works, because of common grace and being in the image of God, these good works do not come from a heart made new and clean (the new nature). The location of the flesh in believers cannot be the same as unbelievers, because of regeneration. The person (soul/spirit) has been born again and given a new nature that is no longer corrupt. This does not mean that the whole person is no longer corrupt. The believer, as a whole person is a combination of a redeemed person and not yet redeemed body (material substance). The flesh refers to the continued location and existence, in this life, of sinful dispositions in the brain/body of the believer.

Human Nature Related Implications

Mapping of the Contours within the Whole Person

Life mentoring provides a more tangible and organized mapping of human nature. By more clearly defining and locating the person as the soul/spirit, people can more readily differentiate and distinguish their person from the processes within the brain. Sin and personal issues can then be viewed from the perspective of not being the deepest desires of the person, but rather the functioning of the brain/body. With the inner sense of detachment from brain/body problematic functioning, the person can then more readily and effectively address these problems of sin and dysfunction. This mapping of the human nature of the whole person relies on biblically-based theological truth, especially regarding the supernatural and permanent change occurring in regeneration.

Providing a more Solid foundation for Hope

When human nature is poorly understood as a muddled, mixture of internal processes, it is difficult for people to get a clear sense of their person apart from contaminated inner processes. When a person is in Christ, this confusion inhibits both a sense of being solidly new in Christ and being perfectly prepared to make progress in life. The effects of regeneration, justification, and sanctification should be understood as providing a solid new person who is enabled by the Holy Spirit to influence the brain and body, thus directing the whole person to being more consistently Christ-like. Seeing oneself in this manner both grounds and increases hope – a hope that one can experience change and in fact will be changed.

Allowing for Choice

The perhaps unintentional consequence of an unclear view of the person versus the brain and body, is to put limitations on the perceived ability to choose. Granted that unbelievers have not been freed from the power of sin, but even so, when unbelievers are able to affirm having an immaterial person they are enabled to identify more readily with an ability to make choices over internal processes and external behaviors of the material part. Believers, having a clear understanding that their persons are distinct from their brain and body functioning, are enabled potentially to an even greater extent to enact the choices that can be made, because of also being freed from the power of sin and empowered by the Holy Spirit.

Greater Sense of Renewal and Salvation

When a person in Christ does not have a well-defined understanding of the extent of the actual supernatural change in regeneration, then the sense of the renewal in salvation is distorted and minimized. With a well-defined and located understanding of human nature, along with a strong view of regeneration, there is an opportunity to more clearly contrast the already new person with the yet to be renewed brain and body. With an enhanced distinction between what is new (soul/spirit) and what is old (brain/body) in the whole person, there can be a greater sense of and confidence in the extent of salvation renewal that has occurred.

Biblical and theological teachings about salvation in Christ can have a ring of abstracted truth that is intellectually acknowledged, but not necessarily personally absorbed. When the internal contours within are clarified to distinguish the inner structure of the human being, then salvation can be identified as a change that is specifically defined and located. Believers can recognize more fully and have a deeper grasp of the work accomplished in salvation − that salvation is a personal change already done in a definite part of oneself, even while still being in process in another definite part of oneself.

More Honesty that Comes from Assurance and Detachment

Hiding imperfect aspects of oneself and behavior from others is a self-protective attempt to keep from being unacceptable to another. This is a form of dishonestly, coming from fear. Hiding from God occurred in the Garden of Eden after disobedience. This hiding is not unlike what people commonly do in relationships. However, if one knows intellectually and personally that there is unconditional acceptance, then there is freedom from the fear of being unacceptable. A strong basis for the courage to be honest can be derived from the assurance of being a fully redeemed and accepted person in Christ, even while still having imperfections in the performance of the brain and body. The identity as a child of God then brings with it an assurance of acceptableness and a willingness to be more honest in the self-assessment of ongoing sinfulness and weakness. Because one can more honestly reveal imperfections when one is secure about being accepted by the other, communication can be more open. With this greater personal awareness and assurance of acceptance, admission of imperfections and confession of the shortcomings can be made more freely, and there can be a fuller cooperation with others toward personal and spiritual growth. This is the case in one's relationship with God as well, where the varied internal sanctification issues can be more extensively and fully addressed.

Clearer Perspective on the Internal Struggle

How can one really know the struggle between the fruit of the Spirit and the works of the flesh, when there is confusion about what parts of oneself are engaged in the conflict? If the person can internally step his/her person back from the fray and view the place where the battle is raging, then there is a valuable perspective from which to move forward and trust in being strengthened (Philippians 4:13). There is a "me" who He will strengthen, and a "we" who will together fight the battle. The believer's battle is understood to be between the person (soul/spirit) and the flesh (in the brain and body), with the person being empowered the Holy Spirit. The believer does not approach the struggle victoriously by saying, "I am the badness I seek to defeat." Rather, the believer approaches the struggle by acknowledging that, "I am the new person enabled to defeat the non-person remaining imperfections."

No denial of Sin and the Impossibility of Perfection in this Life

It is a faulty conclusion to believe that because of the view expressed here of the soul already being perfect in Christ, that what is also being put forth is that Christians don't sin. That is a faulty conclusion because it misses the reality that in this life human beings are whole persons − the soul/spirit embedded in the whole person, together with the yet unredeemed body. Therefore, because of remaining sinful dispositions in the flesh, Christians do continue to sin in this life. The sinning is not because of a continued identity as a sinner (someone outside of an adopted relationship with God through Christ), but because of being a saint who still sins. God has adopted Christians, but their redemption though already accomplished and currently fulfilled in the soul/spirit, is not yet fulfilled in the body. Their body dies and has to undergo a resurrection/transformation.

Location and Reality of Psychological Processes and Problems

As stated previously, the view put forth here is that humans have a material part (the brain and the rest of the body) and an immaterial part (the soul or spirit) to their whole person, and the soul or spirit is the person. Remaining fallenness is understood to reside in the material part, i.e., in the brain and body. This could be misunderstood as saying that since sin has been eradicated, in the person (soul / spirit) by regeneration, then all that remains to be done can be accomplished through psychotherapy – the solution needed to repair the problems remaining in the brain and body. This faulty conclusion may come from a difficulty understanding that there is still a sin problem – validating that even though the soul is already redeemed by regeneration, there is still a need for forgiveness and growth toward Christ-likeness.

There may also be a confusion of what it means to have sin, with what it means to have psychological problems. Psychological problems and their associated psychological processes are also a result of the Fall and are dysfunctions of the brain. These psychological issues and problems (psychopathology) are intangible. They are intangible, but no less real than the dysfunction that comes from a brain disorder like Dementia, Alzheimer's disease, or Schizophrenia.

Sin and psychopathology are two distinct but related conditions (both happening in the physical part of the person) that can impact each other. Not all sin is psychopathology and not all psychopathology is sin, just as not all thoughts and actions of the brain and body are sinful. The body was originally part of God's good creation. Of course, the Fall happened and every imperfection in humankind is a result of this Fall, so it can be said there is no good thing in the whole person. In this sense of separation from God in the Fall, there is nothing good that could be done in the body apart from the redemption in Christ Jesus. This principle is one category of sin – that coming from the Fall. It is of a different category than the category of sinful behaviors. The Bible indicates a distinction between sin as a principle that taints everything in creation and the specific sinful behaviors done by a person, in the body. There is also a Biblical recognition of both sinful and good behaviors that can be done in the body.

Locating the psychological problems in the material brain and body is an important perspective for efficacy both spiritually and psychologically. Personal efficacy means that the person's beliefs and actions, about oneself and resources, are indicating having confidence in the ability to change oneself. There is more empowerment of efficacy when it is understood that one's person is distinct from one's brain and body, and the person can make choices to effect change in the brain and body. Further empowerment for efficacy occurs when believers understand that not only is their person distinct from their brain and body, but that their person has been freed from the power of sin and the Holy Spirit strengthens their person.

Concluding Remarks

There are differing views about what happens in the person and where it happens in the person with regard to regeneration. The view presented here is that there is real supernatural recreation of the soul (the new nature) and that the sinful desires of the old nature still linger in the brain and body (the flesh), but Christians indeed only have one nature − the new nature. Making this clear distinction between soul and body is biblically supported and very helpful for understanding the human role in the process of change, especially Christians changing. By believing in this distinction, it clarifies that one's impact on change (toward more Christ-likeness) can be more effective and one's management of psychological processes more possible. The life mentoring perspective has a real benefit for providing a solid spiritually-based equipping for Christian workers to be ready to positively assist with the personal issues that emerge in the people with whom they are ministering.

Some might question the wisdom and necessity of introducing into life mentoring teachings views that could be considered different from common Christian thinking (i.e., a common Christian thinking that is often underdeveloped regarding a biblical view of human nature and related concepts). However, if the aforementioned definitions and locations were not included in life mentoring, it could be asked, "What new insight or additional contribution does life mentoring make?" The goals of deepening the here-and-now relationship with God and growth in Christ-like virtues are common-fair in assisting others from a Christian perspective. It is the third goal that would be seriously impoverished without the more developed and biblically grounded life mentoring teaching on human nature. To effect change to personal resilience and the management of personal problems, requires a model of the structure and functioning of human nature that is both sound and beyond the commonplace.

The above explanations are provided because there might be questions about where the life mentoring material is coming from both theologically and psychologically. A robust, accurate model of human nature ought to provide for a significant impact on the enhancement of positive psychological functioning and personal resilience. Diligent effort has been put into developing life mentoring from a clarified biblical view of human nature, so that it can better accomplish these personal gains.

The Life Mentor Training Process

Objectives and Overview

Life Mentor Training provides an opportunity for life mentor candidates to explore and understand the process of change and the type of change that is associated with life mentoring. In the life mentoring relationship, the client's personal issues are identified and then these personal issues are addressed by: working toward positive *situational* goals, and also by working on the underlying *life goals* of strengthening the character of the person and having a more here-and-now relationship with God. During training, the *Life in Process*[3] material serves as an example of a common overall progression and typical sequence of change, as experienced when doing life mentoring. The book, with its worksheets, is used as a tool that has helpful examples of ways to use principles and content within meetings, while following a process.

Training Objectives with Explanations

1. Participants will have an enhanced understanding of Life Mentoring through the use of the *Life in Process* material as an illustrative teaching tool.

   - The life mentor training utilizes worksheet material from the book for convenience and to teach concepts, but not an ongoing program for doing life mentoring.

   - Training participants are at the beginning of their life mentoring contact with clients and can benefit from the structure of the material, to help clients tell their stories and focus.

   - Using the structured worksheets, mentors-in-training can more easily focus on their client's primary current concern (story), without having to be self-conscious about practicing listening micro-skills or to struggle with how to run the meetings.

---

[3]   Morgan. *Life in Process.*

2. Participants will be prepared to use the *Life in Process* material for the supervised life mentor practice training.

   - At first, the structured life mentoring worksheets will likely be used in a more mechanical manner, but with practice, the life mentor's style of interacting should become more natural.

   - The development of the life mentor is more through the blending of concepts and principles into the helping style of the life mentor, than through a learned set of procedures to be performed.

3. Participants will learn a basic process of change and the associated principles.

   - The process of life mentoring has three stage-related areas that include the person's story, what the person desires, and taking action.

   - The book content and worksheets take care of focusing the client on particular tasks in each meeting, as well as on the overall process of change.

   - By relying on the worksheet, the life mentor-in-training is freed to better concentrate on listening to the client's story, and to determine related desires and actions, while also learning how to incorporate positive relationship dynamics with God and growth in personal virtues.

4. Participants will receive content and conceptual information related to the encouragement of spiritual and personal growth.

   - The underlying objective of life mentoring is both spiritual and personal — the **life goals**: deepened real-time personal intimacy with God, strengthened virtue-related character, and increased resilience in personal functioning.

- The life mentor works with the client to meet the *situational goals* that are at the same time integrated with the *life goals*.

5. Participants will learn a structured model of helping others to manage personal issues, while not overextending the help beyond the mentor's qualifications.

   - While in training, the life mentor stays close to the material on the worksheets and experiences how it feels to stay within helping boundaries.

6. Participants will receive encouragement to address their own personal and spiritual development during the training.

   - While life mentors are practicing with clients, they receive supervision that will focus not only on the content of the practice meetings, but also on the life mentor's and the client's personal process during the meetings.

   - Though life mentor training is not primarily for the purpose of experiencing or learning how to do spiritual formation, spiritual formation will likely be happening as a result of the process.

7. Through supervision participants will begin to generalize what they have learned· while working with the practice client, to working with other clients and in a less worksheet structured manner.

Life in Process Principles of Change

Life in Process was written to utilize Christian principles from the Twelve Steps to provide content for a general model of personal change. The material can be used in association with primary goals for the relationship, such as discipleship or Bible teaching goals. A temporary break can be taken from that work, so that personal issues can be worked-on. Afterwards, more effective work can be done on the primary goals.

Principles described in *Life in Process* are intended to spark reflection toward pursuing what is being described in each chapter. The chapter content corresponds with exploring the quality of ones relationship with God, considering character qualities and virtues, and managing personal issues within ones relationship with God. The overall goal is movement toward spiritual growth.

Central Organizing Concepts

The central organizing concepts flowing through all the *Life in Process* material are relationship with God as our loving Father and transformation of character. This relationship is the change empowering cohesiveness behind the various principles, constructs, and content of the material. The ever-present question is, "How is God involved with me in this principle and its process?" An adult child and the Father is the defined relationship, though care has to be taken to conform the contours of this relationship to the true character of God (an accurate God image) and the true condition of human nature.

A qualitative change toward a deeper connection to God and strengthened character are here promoted as the primary underlying means for coping with, managing, and transcending life challenges and related personal issues. The mentor's ultimate goal is to promote the strengthening of the person's intimate bond with God and character virtues. Out of this foundation, the individual's necessary personal life changes can be made. Mentors act as a bridge from how the person has been living, to where the person needs to be living with a fuller understanding of and experience of God as a loving Father, who accepts the person on the basis of His grace and not performance.

Mentoring is more a pointing to this life unifying and transforming relationship with God, than it is a resolving of the personal issues in the one being mentored. When the quality of ones real-time relationship with God is improved and the person's character more developed, then the ability to transcend life challenges and suffering is strengthened and established. The increased sense of God's closeness and personal involvement, along with increased self-understanding, character, and conscious or willed change in functioning, increases ones resilience to the circumstances of life. Much work can be done applying principles, such as those in *Life in Process*, but what is experienced in relationship with the mentor and ultimately with God is at the heart of change.

Comments on the Stages and Process of Change in Life Mentoring

The idea of change involving stages is well supported. Secular models show a progression that has beginning, middle, and ending stages. These stages indicate a progression from information gathering and insight formation, to goal setting and on to a working stage where change is attempted and hopefully accomplished.

If one is attempting to assist another in some manner, such as with encouraging or teaching, then there needs to be a way to understand and deal with the other's personal issues. This is the case because personal issues are so frequently present and inevitably surface and interfere with attempts to minister to the person and can hinder the desired ministry outcome (e.g., a deeper understanding of the Bible, a closer relationship with God). How to address these personal issues requires an understanding of a process to strengthen character and deepen intimacy with God – knowing the process from the present condition to a more adequate management of personal problems. When it comes to helping another person and there are personal issues present, then one needs to have an understanding of a process leading toward the managing of these issues or risk being jointly lost in the issues, frustrated – in over ones head and feeling overburdened with the other's problems.

The *Life in Process* material, within a life mentoring relationship, is a way to use Christian principles to walk with another person through a process of change. Change is here defined as the working through of a process that leads to positive progress in the management of personal problems and issues. This positive progress leads to a clearer understanding of ones own issues, a further development in character qualities, and an increased intimacy with God the loving Father that includes the management of ones own issues.

The Dimensions of Change

There are a number of different dimensions that have to be considered when desiring to intentionally and positively influence another person, including personalizing whatever you are attempting to teach or convey. It is naïve, at best, to believe that this influencing will not need to also address, to some extent, personal issues. Personal issues are part of the interpretive context of the person while learning and changing. As such, common stages of change, virtues, relationship, goals, and interventions are all dimensions in the progression of the intentionally influencing relationship. These will all be present, even if unintended, but greater success will be associated with how skillfully these elements are understood and utilized.

Helping as Techniques or Relationship

A valuable way of understanding and teaching psychotherapy is to divide it into two key parts, a technical part and a relational part. The technical portion pertains to the techniques or methods used by the psychotherapist to promote change. The second part pertains to the therapeutic relationship that unfolds between therapist and patient.[4] Life mentoring has this second part, the unfolding of relationship, as of primary importance. In this perspective, the focus is on the life mentor-client relationship, and the life mentor-offered relationship conditions are the most important for change. It is hoped that the life mentoring relationship will point the way more clearly toward the client's relationship with God and provide an experienced relationship consistent with God's way of relating to the person.

---

[4]   Gelso, *Emerging and Continuing Trends in Psychotherapy: Views From an Editor's Eye*, 182–187.

Practical Training Information

As mentioned previously, Life Mentor Training includes a pre-class assignment, an informational class, and two levels of practice with supervision. The pre-class assignment is to read *An Introduction to Life Mentor Training* and become familiar with the *Life in Process* material. The informational class is a one-day Life Mentor Training seminar covering concepts in *An Introduction to Life Mentor Training*. There are two levels of post-class supervised training, requiring participants to use the Life in Process related worksheets and be involved in supervision meetings to discuss the life mentoring process.

Summary Points

Three Life Goals for the focus of Life Mentoring:

1. **Relationship with God**: Improved real-time relating

2. **Growth in virtues**: More Christ-like in character

3. **Better coping and management of personal issues**: Improved Personal Functioning and Flourishing

Three Stages in the Life Mentoring process:

1. **Telling their story** (The Current Picture)

2. **Setting situational goals** (The Preferred Picture)

3. **Taking action** (The Way Forward)

Relationship as the Context for Change:

1. Life mentoring emphasizes relationship as a means to change.

2. The quality of the relationship that the life mentor has with the client contributes significantly to positive growth in real-time relating with God and the development of Christ-like virtues.

The Structure of Human Nature

Introduction to Human Nature and Character Resource Material

This resource material offers a perspective on the internal structure of the person along with the character of the person. When we are talking about the psychological personality and change, we are talking about personality functioning changing. When we are talking about the person and character, we are talking something happening related to human nature and virtues. Human nature is the category for study that focuses on what we mean when we use the term, person, and character is here believed to be the functioning of the composite of virtues within the person that we have labeled as character. Since life mentoring is focused directly on the person and change in character, we will here be exploring what a person is, and how character, with its virtues, is related to the person.

But, let us pause for a moment and consider, why would a life mentor need to explore the meaning of human nature? An understanding of human nature is an essential and foundational staring point when attempting to assist another person to change. Here's a simple illustration of the need to have an accurate view of human nature. I have been a licensed driver for nearly 50 years. Most of those years were in the US, with US drivers licenses, but now I live in Austria and also have an Austrian driver's license – so far so good. Now here is the comparison that highlights the problem. While driving in Austria, I could make right turns on red stoplights indefinitely. So what's the problem? The problem is that making a right turn on a red light does not conform to Austrian law. Driving that way in Austria works, but it is in violation of a law that may not come into play unless certain things happen – in this case, if the Polizei see me making an illegal turn. I can use the US driving rules in Austria, but I am doing so incorrectly. To drive legally, I need to conform to Austrian laws. Similarly, I can have the wrong view of human nature and go along fine for an indefinite period of time, but what happens if I get "caught" in some manner. I will experience that my faulty or inadequate view of human nature is not following the rules, and I will suffer the consequences or my clients will.

There are a variety of views regarding human nature. Broadly speaking, there are views that consider humans to be of one or more than one substance. Human nature is here being used to identify the structure of the person — the meta-design. Human nature is either composed of only a physical or material substance, or both a material and an immaterial substance. In the makeup of substances, human nature is either monistic, dualistic, or a combination.

As we begin this discussion of human nature, here are some points to keep in mind that emphasize the importance of having an understanding of human nature, for either psychology and counseling, or in our case life mentoring.

When Considering the Human Nature[5]

- The inner being ("soul") and human nature have been ongoing topics of interest historically.

- There is a wide range of opinions about human nature — the human person, each with its own assumptions and implications.

- Psychology and counseling are focused on knowing and assisting human beings, therefore attempts should be made toward a clearer understanding of human nature.

- What we believe about human nature is going to impact how we approach the understanding and resolution of human problems.

- For reasons similar to those for psychology and counseling, spiritual transformation also needs to be grounded in a well-defined view of human nature.

---

[5]   Beck & Demarest, *The Human Person in Theology and Psychology*, 163.

Human Nature Relevance[6]

- "...any discipline or inquiry that seeks to study humans must begin that study with an examination of these two foundational issues: Is the human person composed of one substance or two or more substances."

- "Psychologists and other social scientists who deal with these issues do not, however, organize their investigations around scriptural categories."

- "Thus we will not find listings in the indexes of psychological volumes for 'Image of God' or 'soul.' Yet we find psychological material directly related..."

- "Modern psychology primarily has dealt with the issue of whether humans consist of one or more substances in an indirect manner. More often than not, the issue is implied or assumed rather than explicated [analyzed and developed] by psychological investigators."

- Philosophy is the primary discipline discussing the mind-body problem (MBP).

- "Well-trained psychologists may receive training in the history and philosophy of psychology, but more often than not these topics receive only cursory attention in psychological training programs."

We will begin with a discussion of human nature's composition and functioning and then explore more specifically the soul as being the real person. This will be followed by material on the human situational context and the will to make changes with reference to character.

---

6   Ibid., 163-164.

One Nature[7]

Humans are here considered as only being capable of having one nature at a time. Contrary to the popular, but mistaken Christian view that Christians have a new nature and a sinful nature after becoming a Christian, there is still only one nature. The unbeliever has an old or sinful nature and the born again believer has a new nature. The unbeliever is identified as a "sinner" and the believer is identified as a "saint" who sins, due to remaining sinful desires.

The human situation in general is a continuation of the situation of Adam and Eve after the Fall. The personal identity or the self is not-able-to-not-sin. I say in general because there is an altered condition of mankind. This is the other condition or situation of human persons who have undergone a justification done by God. This justification is available by faith. The person is "born again" or regenerated—a re-creation of the inner person or soul. This is referred to as the new man. The prior sinful nature is replaced by a new nature. We will be spending more time focusing on this person who has left the situation of being unregenerate and is now in a restored relationship with God.

Murray, regarding Romans 6:1–11, states the following:

> 'Our old man' is the old self or ego, the unregenerate man in his entirety in contrast with the new man as the regenerate in his entirety. It is a mistake to think of the believer as both old man and a new man or as having in him both the old man and the new man, the latter in view of regeneration and the former because of remaining corruption. [8]

He is saying that the old man was crucified once and for all and that there is a breach with sin that occurs through union with Christ. So what explains the continuance of sin in the Christian life?

---

7   Much of this section is adapted from: Morgan, *The soul that suffers: A perspective on human nature and suffering for counseling Christians,* chapter 3.

8   Murray, *The Epistle to the Romans,* 219–220.

Stott[9] states that our souls are redeemed but not our bodies, and it is our unredeemed bodies that cause us to groan. His view is that our fallen sinful disposition dwells in our mortal bodies. It is important to distinguish between the inward and the outward person. Ladd refers to this:

> Paul uses the phrase *ho eso anthropos* in two different ways: of the unregenerate person and of the regenerate person. In Romans 7:22, the 'inmost self' is used synonymously with 'mind,' which can approve the Law of God and will to obey it, but finds itself impotent. Behm describes this as 'the spiritual side of man, or man himself in so far as he enjoys self-awareness, as he thinks and wills and feels.' In 2 Corinthians 4:16, the inner person is contrasted with the 'outer person'—the human as a corruptible earthy being. While the outward person is wasting away, the inner one is being renewed every day. 'The inward man is the real self that passes from the body of flesh to the body of resurrection.' In both instances, 'the inner man' is the higher, essential self, either redeemed or redeemable, made for God and opposed to sin.

> The 'old man' denotes 'the sinful being of the unconverted man.' The important thing to note is the tension between the indicative and the imperative: the old person—the old nature—the old self has been put to death—it has been put off in principle. Paul does not say that sin is dead but that the believer has died to sin. He does not say that the flesh is done away, but that we no longer live in the flesh and therefore are not to walk according to the flesh. He never says, 'Do not sin,' but rather, 'Do not let sin reign over you.'[10]

9　　Stott, *Men Made New*, 96.
10　　Ladd, *A Theology of the New Testament*, 519.

Ladd goes on to say that, "While the flesh has been crucified with Christ in principle, it can still be an active power in the Christian's life and he or she must be constantly vigilant to keep the flesh under the control of the Spirit."[11]

This[12] clarification that there are not two natures in the Christian, but rather a new nature and remaining sinful dispositions, is a significant issue. The body (which includes the brain) has not yet been fully redeemed, though being in the process of sanctification. Murray writes about this with reference to Romans 6:19: "the emphasis falls upon the once-for-all breach with sin and commitment to righteousness."[13] The sinful dispositions still remain in the body, with its brain. Murray clarifies this distinction between the person and what remains to be changed in the body, in his comments on Romans 6:13.

> If "mortal body" [verse 12] means the physical organism, then the "members" referred to in this verse [verse 13] must mean the members of the body, such as eye, hand, and foot. Sin is conceived of as a master at whose disposal we place these members in order that they may be instruments to promote unrighteousness. The exhortation is to the effect that we are not to go on placing our physical organs at the disposal of sin for the furtherance of such an end. The positive counterpart is that we are to present ourselves to God as those alive from the dead and our members as instruments of righteousness to God. This fuller statement shows that although the thought had been concentrated upon the bodily (vss. 12, 13a), yet the apostle does not regard the physical as comprehending the sum-total of devotion. Believers are to present *themselves* to God as those

---

[11] Ibid., 536-537.
[12] The material in the remainder of this section has been taken from: Morgan, *The Soul as the Person Who Experiences the Brain's Psychological Functioning*, 45-53.
[13] Murray, *The Epistle to the Romans*, 234.

alive from the dead. Here the whole personality is in view....We are regarded as presenting ourselves and our members once for all to God for his service and the promotion of righteousness.[14]

The person is here being portrayed as the agent who is able to direct the body (brain included) toward that which is righteous. When person is referred to, the reference is to someone who is present and other than the material body. This other-than-material-person is free to choose to move the body in a righteous direction. This concept, of the person being able to direct the body, is directly applicable to counseling. The person in counseling or life mentoring is then capable of impacting the functioning of his or her body, which would include the psychological functioning of the brain. As the brain's psychological functioning improves, significant barriers to sanctification are being removed.

Two Parts to a Whole Person[15]

Before we proceed any further, some terms need to be defined.[16] The issue of understanding human nature will be addressed by focusing on the mind-body problem (though some may think it more accurately described as the personal identity problem). Mind will here be defined as referring to the nonmaterial aspect of the person, and will here be considered as interchangeable with the terms soul, spirit, person, and self. This is consistent with Evans[17] use of such terms more or less synonymously "to refer to whatever a person refers to when that person uses the term, 'I' to refer to himself or herself as a conscious agent." The term body will be used in reference to the

---

14   Ibid., 227-228.

15   This section is adapted from: Morgan, *The soul that suffers: A perspective on human nature and suffering for counseling Christians*, chapter 3.

16   This paragraph is taken from: Morgan, "The Soul as the Person Who Experiences the Brain's Psychological Functioning."

17   Evans, "Separable Souls: Dualism, Selfhood, and the Possibility of Life After Death," 330.

material or physical aspect of the person. Berkhof[18] states that the usual view is that man consists in two parts, body and soul, and that biblically "the two words 'soul' and 'spirit' are used interchangeably." The positions that are referred to as materialistic monism, dualism, and holistic dualism are also relevant to this discussion. Cooper's[19] definitions will be used. Regarding monism, Cooper states, "For the materialistic monist, a person or soul is the set of human mental capacities generated by the human body and brain--a 'mentating' or 'personating' organism." Cooper[20] defines dualism--one that is consistent with the biblical text--as meaning a dichotomy of ego and the earthly organism such that "we can survive 'coming apart' at death, unnatural as this may be." Finally, Cooper's[21] definition of dualism "does not require viewing the body and soul as self-contained, independently functioning entities, at least not during earthly life." His understanding of the dualism of biblical anthropology is that it is actually a functional holism (a holistic dualism). Holistic dualism is the view adopted here.

The affect of what we believe about ourselves is one reason why I am concerned about our views of human nature. A monistic view that says people are only a whole person, clouds the distinctness and the reality of the regenerate inner being who is able to have an influence on the rest of the person. Apart from taking away the hope of having a separable "soul" that goes to be with the Lord immediately at death, a monistic view can trap Christians in a belief that they are only whole persons, apparently having no solid new person within them. The person in a monistic viewpoint seems to have endless layers of deeper and deeper psychological processes organized into a whole person, but no distinct already redeemed person who can have some measure of control.

---

[18] Berkhof, *A Summary of Christian Doctrine,* 61.
[19] Cooper, *Body, Soul, and Life Everlasting,* 165.
[20] Ibid., 163.
[21] Ibid., 164.

The view promoted here is of the person as being both material and immaterial. This could be thought of as a type of dichotomous view or dualism. Though some may see this as naive or indefensible based on the meaning of New Testament words such as soul and spirit, or because of the influence of Greek ideas, there is a plain reading of texts that indicates an existence of the person immediately after this life — a personal existence both in and apart from the body. (Please refer to Grudem's[22] chapter on the essential nature of man for a fuller explanation of the Scriptural basis for soul or spirit and body, as well as for the existence of the immaterial part of a person after death.)

I use the term "inner being" or "soul" to refer to the immaterial person and the term "whole person" to mean the entire person immaterial and material. I use the term "personality" to refer to the mental functioning of the brain. Humans do function as a unified whole and the ultimate eternal state for Christians is not to be bodiless, but to receive a transformed body. (If you are interested in a historical review on the discussion of human nature, let me recommend Berkouwer[23], though with the caution that he does not hold to a dichotomous view. Additionally, Goetz and Taliaferro have written on the history of the soul.[24])

Why would I take the position of emphasizing an immaterial person— the soul—as being distinct (not separate) from the body and the whole person? To begin with, I think this position is consistent with a New Testament biblical perspective. Jesus refers to belief in an immaterial soul-person in His statement to the thief on the cross that he (this "person") would be with Him in Paradise that very day (Luke 23:43). It is also consistent with the Apostle Paul's desire to depart from the body and be at home with the Lord (Philippians 1:22—24). In both situations a "person" would exist apart from the body after death. Why is this position important to our discussion? It fits the mindset of most conservative Christians, who naturally

---

[22] Grudem, *Systematic Theology: An Introduction to Biblical Doctrine*, 472—489.
[23] Berkouwer, *Man: The Image of God*, 194—233.
[24] Goetz & Taliaferro, *A Brief History of the Soul*.

believe in an immaterial person that exists after death. Having this assurance is also significant for having peace in this life.

The Soul as the Person[25]

A holistic dualism can assert that there is a nonmaterial aspect to a person, a soul, and that there is a material brain and a material body, with the nonmaterial and material working together as a unified whole. However, rather than the material brain itself being the originator of human consciousness, it could just as well be understood that the nonmaterial soul animates the brain to produce consciousness and other brain functions, including psychological functions. In this line of thinking, the brain becomes a sort of transmitter or reducing valve. Beauregard and O'Leary [26] describe this in their agreement "with William James's hypothesis that the brain does not generate but transmits and expresses mental processes/events. From this perspective, the brain can be compared with a television receiver that translates electromagnetic waves (which exist apart from the TV receiver) into picture and sound."[27] They go on to state that, "Along similar lines, Henri Bergson and Aldous Huxley have proposed that our brains do not produce mind and consciousness, but rather act as reducing valves, allowing us the experience of only a narrow portion of perceivable reality. This outlook implies that the brain normally limits our experience of the spiritual world."[28] Berkhof, in a discussion of the future intermediate state, also comments on the present life, "From the fact that the human consciousness in the present life transmits its effect through the brain, it does not necessarily follow that it can work in no other way."[29]

---

[25] The material in this section has been taken from: Morgan, *The Soul as the Person Who Experiences the Brain's Psychological Functioning*, 45-53.
[26] Beauregard and O'Leary, *The Spiritual Brain*.
[27] Ibid., 292.
[28] Ibid., 292-293.
[29] Berkhof, *Systematic Theology*, 688.

From a human perspective, without the Scriptures to inform, the brain appears to be the source of conscious experience. However, a materialist attempting to explain human conscious experience is much like a person trying to get into the experience of a bat using sonar. Even more difficult, it seems, would be a materialist attempting to understand the experience of a regenerate believer in Jesus Christ. An understanding of this regeneration is dependent upon what is revealed in the Scriptures.

The soul as the person who is experiencing the brain's psychological functioning is a concept that can now be summarized and applied to Christian psychotherapy and life mentoring. This concept draws a distinction between the nonmaterial (the soul/person) and the material (the brain and the rest of the physical body), yet affirms that there is also one whole person--the embodied personal identity. The soul of the regenerate believer has been redeemed having godly dispositions, a determinate will to please God, and the empowering work of the Holy Spirit. The soul is strengthened by the encouragement of virtue development, as in life mentoring.

The brain is understood to retain all its neural functioning and the rest of the body it's functioning, but both are still corrupted by sin and in need of redemption (sanctification). The person as a whole still sins, but there is a process within the whole person, from the soul outward, that is moving this whole person in the direction of increasing Christlikeness, first in character and then in actions.

However, psychological and biological treatments are also retained within this holistic dualism view of human nature, since the brain and body are still suffering − still in need of being redeemed. There are still those occasions when there is a necessity for a Christian psychotherapy, but one that is informed by a biblical and theological understanding of human nature, while at the same time being informed as well by a psychology and biology kept in perspective by this understanding of human nature.

The Functioning
of Human Nature

Human Nature and Corruption[30]

To define personal identity requires us to also consider the context of the human situation. By human situation, I mean not only the contexts culturally, relationally, and in terms personal functioning, but also the historical context of what it means to have a personal identity. We will here be focused on clarifying the foundational historical context in which to situate personal identity. Evolution provides many people with a context. Conclusions about the human person are developed accordingly. This is not the orientation of our historical context. Rather, ours will focus on the biblical and historical facts of the story of the Creation and Fall of mankind.

It should be of no surprise that a Christian account of the history of personal identity would return to the Garden of Eden. When God created Adam and Eve, He created them in His image. Much has been made of what it means to be in the image of God. There are differing views and emphases. Some would say that to be in the image of God means that humans are relational, and others would emphasize the human rational abilities as image bearers—to be able to think as God thinks, though of course within human limitations. One thing that is clear from the Genesis account is that man was formed physically out of elements from the Earth, but then breathed into by God. There were two necessary conditions: one material from the Earth and one spiritual from God. This is foundational to our understanding. We will take a traditional Christian perspective that since creation mankind has been composed of both that which is material and that which is immaterial. However, while being both material and immaterial, humans are also considered here to be whole persons. This is just one case of the wide spread occurrence of the one-and-the-many that we see throughout creation and in God as well.

---

[30] This section is adapted from: Morgan, *The soul that suffers: A perspective on human nature and suffering for counseling Christians*, Chapter 3.

It was in the Garden that our original parents were created, lived, and became disobedient to the instructions they had been given by God. We have no personal experience that would help us to fully relate to what life was like for Adam and Eve in their pre-Fall condition. They were in a condition in which they were free to choose either good or evil. Before the Fall there was no inner conflict between the material and the immaterial. Adam and Eve were fully integrated in body and soul. As Robertson[31], in discussing the Covenants of Works and Grace, points-out, Adam cannot be regarded as a purely mythical figure. There was a real relationship between God and man; one that pre-Fall required perfect obedience as the meritorious ground of blessing.

By contrast, we are very familiar with the post-Fall consequences. Gangel establishes the origin of conflict in the Garden with the following explanation:

> From Genesis to Revelation God tells us about conflict. Originally, Adam and Eve were created without conflict as a part of their experience. By Genesis 3, sin had become a part of the human dilemma. Conflict immediately surfaced on at least five levels:
>
> 1.   No longer could Adam and Eve fellowship with their Creator....
>
> 2.   The seeds of interpersonal conflict came to harvest very rapidly as Adam quickly shifted responsibility to Eve.
>
> 3.   Creation or nature would not be productive as it was in the past....
>
> 4.   The spiritual conflict between human beings, Satan, and his organization was set into motion....

---

[31]   Robertson, *The Christ of the Covenants*, 55.

5. Perhaps the most insidious conflict was the internal one. Now Adam and Eve and all their offspring would face the struggle or conflict on the inside created by sin....

The confrontation between sin and righteousness provides a foundational perspective for understanding the history of the Old Testament. From the time God selected Israel to be a special people—through their entrance and exit from Egypt, the conquest of the promised land, the earthly kings who ruled, the captivity and return— the record consistently reveals the message of conflict. Often this conflict was mismanaged, but at no time did God fail to control it. The wisdom literature of the Old Testament illustrates how God provided for a people who demonstrated conflict at the different levels....[32]

But why would Adam and Eve disobey? Calvin aptly describes what was behind Adam and Eve's actions.

Wherefore, the commencement of the ruin in which the human race was overthrown was a defection from the command of God.... But as God does not manifest himself to men otherwise than through the word, so neither is his majesty maintained, nor does his worship remain secure among us any longer than while we obey his word. Therefore, unbelief was the root of defection; just as faith alone unites us to God. For truly they did exalt themselves against God, when, honour having been divinely conferred upon them, they, not content with such excellence, desired to know more than was lawful, in order that they might become equal to God.... If anyone prefers a shorter explanation, we may say unbelief has opened the door to ambition, but ambition has proved

---

[32] Gangel, *Communication and Conflict Management*, 155–156.

that parent of rebellion, to the end that men, having cast aside the fear of God, might shake off his yoke.[33]

They were, however, also prompted toward this rebellion. "The fallen devil (Lu. 10:18) instilled the craving to be as gods into Adam and Eve (Gn. 3:5), with the result that man's entire nature was infected with pride through the Fall (cf. Rom. 1:21-23). Hence we find a sustained condemnation of human arrogance throughout the Old Testament, especially in the Psalms and Wisdom Literature."[34]

Even with the prideful, defiant turn toward self and away from their pure relationship with God, the situation was not hopelessly lost. God began to put his plan into place to restore the destroyed relationship with his creation in general and with human kind in particular. "At that point in history [at the Fall] God and humans turned in different directions. Humans pursued the path of pride and self-concern. God pursued the path of redemptive love."[35]

Adam and Eve chose to break a rule that had been put in place by God. Their existence of full integration and unhindered relationship with each other and God was then permanently changed. They were changed internally and became dis-integrated because of their disobedience. Negative emotions and inner conflict began to be experienced. At the deepest level—in their personal identity— Adam and Eve were no longer free of the power of sin and able to choose to do good, to not sin. However, they were still in the image of God, though reflecting God's image very imperfectly. We can relate to Adam and Eve's condition after the Fall—their 'fallenness'. Their disobedience was sin that set the whole human race at odds with God through a separation from Him. This is still the condition for humans who have not been regenerated by God. He is perfectly righteous and people have to also be perfectly righteous, without sin, in order to be in relationship with Him.

---

[33] Calvin, *Genesis*, 1:153–154.
[34] *The New Bible Dictionary*, 1027.
[35] Mounce, *Romans*, 141.

The Soul and Regeneration[36]

The supernatural event of regeneration (the new birth), of the person who then believes in Jesus Christ as Savior, produces an altered and unique human experience. To attempt a materialist understanding of the regenerate believer's human experience is similar to the difficulty in the analogy mentioned above, of a sighted person trying to understand what a bat experiences using its sonar.[37] Just as the sighted person assumes and imposes his sighted experience when trying to understand the bat, the materialist assumes and imposes his understanding upon the regenerate person. This type of understanding will not account for what is actually occurring. Johnson stated this very clearly. "But to try to understand the redeemed self, the Christian community will, for obvious reasons, receive no help from secularists, since study of the redeemed self can only proceed from a science rooted in regeneration itself ...open to special revelation, which describes the redeemed self in some inspired detail."[38] Johnson goes on to make the statement that "the Christian community must go to the scriptures to find out what the consummated self will look like."[39] There has been a dramatic change to the soul in regeneration and what follows is also characterized by an intimate and empowering connection with God.

We can understand from this that the soul has been made holy, but there still remains the need for further change in the whole person. Stott states that not one of us is wholly saved yet and then clarifies this further.

> Our souls are redeemed, it is true, but not our bodies. And it is our unredeemed bodies which cause us to groan. Why

---

[36] The material in the remainder of this section has been taken from: Morgan, The Soul as the Person Who Experiences the Brain's Psychological Functioning, 45-53.

[37] Nagel, "What is it Like to be a Bat?," 159-168.

[38] Johnson, "Describing the Self within Redemptive History," 20-21.

[39] Ibid., 21.

is this? For one thing, these bodies are weak, fragile and mortal, subject to fatigue, sickness, pain and death. It is this that the apostle has in mind in 2 Corinthians 5:2, 4 when he says that in this body "we groan." But it is also that the "flesh," our fallen sinful nature, dwells in our mortal bodies, "sin which dwells in me" ([Romans] 7:17, 20). Indeed, it is this very indwelling sin which causes us to cry out, "Wretched man that I am! Who will deliver me from this body of death?" Such a shout of anguish is precisely what Paul means by our present inward groaning, except that there the inward groan is audibly expressed.[40]

Here a point of clarification is made that there is a redemption accomplished in the soul, but there remains to be a redemption of the body – keeping in mind that the person as a whole is understood as still sinning.

---

[40] Stott, *Men Made New*, 96.

Life Mentoring and Virtue Development

Growth in the Soul's Virtues

The Context for Virtue-Based Change [41]

The biblical perspective on persons is that there is more to the whole person than what is physical. The biblical historical origin of this view about there being an immaterial dimension to people is traced back to the creation of Adam and Eve. God created them as material bodies with immaterial souls, in perfect unity. Their natures and the character of their natures were originally in a perfect, sinless harmony and in harmony with their physical bodies. Their original intra and inter-personal condition was radically different than that experienced by humans since.

The fall of Adam and Eve — the original evil — was a disobedience to God in the Garden of Eden. It is the explanation for all suffering, from the suffering of all mankind to the suffering of the whole creation. Adam and Eve's disobedience toward God was undergirded by their pride. This is evil in its primary sense. Out of that primary evil, all human suffering has been derived. What we call the consequences of their sin was God's penalty for their sin. All this must be unpacked and mined in order to understand the issue of developing virtues. From our vantage point, this side of the Fall, a biblical view of human nature needs to provide an understanding of how a person is capable of evil and yet can be capable of overcoming evil, thus changing the consequences and reducing suffering wherever possible.

In the case of life mentoring, it is hoped that the immaterial soul of the mentor and the soul of the client, both being mediated by their respective brains and bodies, will connect in a manner such that positive change is possible. In the special case of Christians, whose human natures have been altered through regeneration, an explanation of the born-again human nature must factor-in

---

[41]   This section is adapted from: Morgan, *The soul that suffers: A perspective on human nature and suffering for counseling Christians*, Chapter 2.

the effects and implications of being regenerated by the Holy Spirit. When a person is born-again, the human nature is changed. Having the soul supernaturally made new necessarily requires an additional understanding of this condition of human nature. Christian persons are very much in a different condition from those whose souls have not been regenerated. This understanding of the new birth can then be utilized in the life mentoring relationship and with regard to the current discussion becomes a basis for understanding virtue development.

The view of the immaterial soul — the real person within the whole person and as actually being mediated by the physical brain and body — is a particular view of human nature. Further, that this soul is capable of affecting change in the brain and the rest of the physical body, is an additional distinction. Unfortunately psychologists, even Christian psychologists, have not done a good job of clarifying a view of human nature. Brugger, in his article *Anthropological Foundations*, makes a case for the importance of articulating a normative account of human nature for clinical psychology. He states that, "Most underlying conceptions of human nature in psychology are unacknowledged or unelaborated."[42] I would agree with the author about the importance of clinical psychology defining its view of human nature. I believe it is even more important for Christian psychologists, counselors, and life mentors.[43]

A Christian account of human nature should consider the biblically defined condition of humans as being under a curse apart from Christ. God laid down a standard, the Law, but humans could not fulfill it in order to redeem themselves.

---

42 Brugger, "Anthropological Foundations," 3–15.
43 For a book combining psychological and theological views of human nature, please see Beck and Demarest, *The Human Person in Theology and Psychology*. There is much that can be gained from their exploration of the human person.

For Paul, Christ was the 'end' (*telos*) of the law precisely because he brought to fruition and completion what the law itself could not do (Romans 10:4). This he did by bearing the curse of the law that had justly fallen on everyone who had not fulfilled 'everything written the book of the law.' Thus only in the light of Jesus Christ can we understand either the true nature of humanity as God intended it to be or the radical character of human rebellion in this fallen world. It is not so much that we must paint the world as dark as possible in order to illuminate the glory of Christ; rather it is only in the light of Calvary that we grasp fully, insofar as God grants to us mortals the ability to understand such mysteries, the holiness of God, the horror of sin, and the depth of divine grace that caused all three to meet in a man on a tree.[44]

Once a person is in Christ and redeemed from the curse of the Law, the Holy Spirit begins his sanctifying work — the formation of Christ-like virtues. The re-creating work of the Holy Spirit regenerates the soul. This person then cooperates with the Holy Spirit to transform the problems and sinful dispositions in the physical part of his/her whole person — a progressive overcoming of the corruption in the brain and body of the whole person. Regarding this illumination. Grudem agrees with the view that the Holy Spirit enables Christians generally to understand, to recall to mind, and to apply the Scriptures they have studied.[45] The result of this illuminating work is the production of the fruit of the Spirit in the person—the establishment of the virtues of Christ.

When we are talking about developing virtues, it is important to have this further clarified picture of human nature and how it functions. When we understand that within us is an eternal, spiritual inner being—the soul, then we are clearer about how to view our shortcomings and how to change them. The soul is not the location of psychological problems (nor, in believers, the part of the person with sinful desires). The soul is distinct and from

---

[44]   George, *Galatians*, 231.
[45]   Grudem, *Systematic Theology*, 1041–1042.

this distinct perspective, can make choices. Choice is possible for both those who have been regenerated and those who have not. However, those who have not been regenerated, though having the ability to grow in virtues, do not have their souls cleansed or purified, have not been freed from the power of sin, and do not have the strengthening of the Holy Spirit.

For those who are in-Christ, the true person is a regenerated soul, with the ability to exert influence over their brains and bodies to a greater extent than those persons not regenerated. This ability to transform proceeds out from our soul and it's developing virtuous character as long as the person is physically alive. The regenerated soul is already perfect, even while being in the process of developing the virtues of Christ—Christ-like character. The whole person (soul and body combined) is in the process of becoming holy – a change positively facilitated by the strengthened character of the soul.

When the physical part of the whole person dies, the immaterial person (soul) goes to be with the Lord, but in this life in the physical body, the soul is every bit as real – a real person in the whole person, soul and body. This perspective is encouraging in a manner similar to the encouragement we can have by recognizing that even if we are absent from the body, we are with the Lord (see 2 Corinthians 5:8; Philippians 1:23).

Even secular psychology is beginning to understand that psychology needs to reconnect with an emphasis on character or virtue formation. Martin Seligman is a professor at the University of Pennsylvania and former president of the American Psychological Association. In making his case to renew the focus on virtues, he looks back at the "rock-bottom assumptions held by most educated minds of mid-nineteenth century America:

That there is a human 'nature'

That action proceeds from character

That character comes in two forms, both equally fundamental—bad character, and good or virtuous ('angelic') character"[46]

These are not new or surprising from a Christian perspective, but they are significant when coming from someone within the psychological community. He goes on to say that, "Because all of these assumptions have almost disappeared from the psychology of the twentieth century, the story of their rise and fall is the backdrop for renewing the notion of good character as a core assumption of Positive Psychology."[47] Seligman's Positive Psychology is a notable exception to those who either criticize or ignore the importance of character and virtues. He believes "that the time has come to resurrect character as a central concept to the scientific study of human behavior."[48]

The Will to Change

When talking about the inner being, with the strengthening of the Holy Spirit, changing brain and body functioning, we are at the critical and very practical point of application. How does the inner being actually influence the brain and body? In counseling there is an assumption that the person has a self-system that makes him capable of having a measure of control over his thoughts, feelings, motivation, and actions (self-efficacy). When I am helping a client take action to change, I am trying to assist him to have more control over his brain functions and bodily actions. In other words, I am trying to encourage him to use the will of his inner being to take control over the will of the brain, the psychological will. Murray helps us to understand these two different human wills in the context of explaining Paul's statements in Romans 7:14-25. "It would appear to be that the apostle is using the word 'will' throughout this passage, when he speaks both of what he does will and of what he does not will, in the highly restricted sense of that determinate will to do

---

[46] Seligman, *Authentic Happiness*, 125–129.
[47] Ibid., 125-129.
[48] Ibid., 125-129.

good, in accordance with the will of God, which is characteristic of his deepest and inmost self, the will of 'the inward man' (vs. 22)."[49]

I would interpret Murray to be calling the inner being's will the "determinate" will. He goes on to say that, "It is that will that is frustrated by the flesh and indwelling sin. And when he [Paul] does the evil he does what is not the will of his deepest and truest self, the inward man. This explains both types of expression, namely, that what *he wills* he does not do and what *he does not will* he does." Murray is saying that will in the psychological sense is present in the practice and performance which Paul calls evil. This psychological will is in conflict with his inner being's determinate will. This is not to say that the psychological will is always completely evil. The person, as a Christian, is in the process of becoming more like Christ (sanctification), but there are still the old sin tendencies even while there is positive growth. The hope is that spiritual transformation is happening in which the psychological will is becoming progressively more conformed to the determinate will.

When I share this view of human nature with my Christian clients, they readily understand and appreciate the distinction in wills. Further, they are encouraged to know that they are each an inner being that has been made new and who desires to please God. They are then more aware that they can work with the Holy Spirit to change their whole person. This subtle perspective of detachment, from the brain and body, is important to avoid a sense of being a victim to their own physical processes.[50] The distinction is between the two wills and the emphasis is on the determinate will of inner being (soul-person) as having dominance. It is an encouragement for the client or person being comforted to see herself as already perfect in Christ in her true person, freed from the power of sin, and as already possessing a measure of control

---

49   Murray, *The Epistle to the Romans*, 272.
50   This detachment idea is consistent with *self-distancing external observer perspective* that reduces the duration of negative emotions (Verduyn, et.al., 2012; Shepherd, et.al., 2016).

over the psychological will of the flesh—a Holy Spirit empowered and self-cooperating efficacy (Appendix B on Detachment Steps).

Christian clients need to become aware that they are regenerated in their persons, their souls, even while they are continuing onward in the sanctification process. As for the regenerate part of the person and progressive sanctification, Reymond references the Westminster Confession[51] when he talks about the war between the flesh and the Spirit. "In which war, although the remaining corruption, for a time, may much prevail; yet through the continual supply of strength from the sanctifying Spirit of Christ, the regenerate part doth overcome; and so the saints grow in grace, perfecting holiness in the fear of God."[52]

Although translated from Satan's family into God's, we still bear within us sinful dispositions.[53] The person who has undergone regeneration by God has been changed at the level of the immaterial inner person or soul. At the point of regeneration this inner person is freed from the power of sin, made righteous in God's eyes and is recreated. This is a creative work done by God on the personal identity, the deepest and truest self, the soul. From that point forward there is a split in the whole person between this new self and the sinful tendencies that remain in the flesh.

The personal identity of sinner (being pre-eminently sinful) is incongruent with the new birth. When a person is born, there is a personal identity that results. When a person is born again, there is a personal identity change from sinner to saint, and from orphan to child of God because of adoption by God. An identity as a sinner (one who is pre-eminently sinful) is not the same as the identity of a saint (one who is re-born and a child of God) who still sins.

Sinful tendencies are still in the material part of the person, and

---

[51] *Westminster Confession of Faith*, XIII, 1-3.
[52] Reymond, *A New Systematic Theology*, 767.
[53] Girardeau, *Discussions of Theological Questions*, 478-479.

after the new birth this flesh is in conflict with the deepest and true person (the soul). This conflict is because of having been freed from the power of sin and having the strengthening of the Holy Spirit, but still struggling with the sinful dispositions that are in the brain and body. In the sanctifying work of the Holy Spirit, God is addressing this conflict. But, in this earthly life there is always some remaining sin. It is only in the glorified state, after life here on Earth, that Christians are completely free of and unable to sin.

The[54] regenerate believer, being a person in a body, is capable of having a measure of control over thoughts, feelings, motivation, and actions (a kind of self-efficacy). The person is to move in the direction of having more control over brain functions and bodily actions. As previously mentioned, Murray helps us to understand this as there being two different human wills and does this explaining in the context of Paul's statements in Romans 7:14-25. Murray is calling the soul's will the "determinate will."[55]

Spiritual transformation is happening in which the person's soul, empowered by the Holy Spirit (Ephesians 3:16), is taking more control over the brain's psychological will and out of this flows more godly actions by the rest of the body. This understanding of the regenerate believer — of the determinate will of the person versus the psychological will of the brain — is a concept that can be utilized in Christian psychotherapy and life mentoring. Use of this concept allows the therapist to align appropriately with the client to address the problems in the psychological functioning of the brain. This concept also clarifies that the life mentor is aligning with the determinate will of the person to grow-in and to practice virtues that will promote development in the character of the person.

---

[54] The material in the remainder of this section has been taken from: Morgan, *The Soul as the Person Who Experiences the Brain's Psychological Functioning*, 45-53.

[55] Murray, *The Epistle to the Romans*, 272.

Summary Points

The Structure of Human Nature and Life Mentoring:

1. Human Beings have both material (brain and the rest of the body) and immaterial (the soul or actual person) parts to the whole person.

2. The soul animates and exerts influence over the brain and the rest of the body.

3. This view of the soul is essential for understanding life mentoring's intention to align with the dominant will of soul of the client in order to influence the psychological will of the brain — a process of a healthy detachment of the person from his or her problems.

Virtues as a Resource for Change

Life mentoring is a way to improve the resilience of the person to life challenges, such that there is improved personal functioning. This is accomplished through a relationship in which virtues are encouraged, as is a deepening relationship with God. Even though the outcome is improved personal functioning, the focus is not directly on psychological factors. (This not having to deal with psychological issues may be a relief for some life mentors, but not exploring these issues may be disappointment for others who are intrigued by psychological processes.)

In our therapeutically minded western cultural context, it may seem like psychology rules the person, so helping at its highest and best is brought about through psychotherapy. For this to be the case, one has to have already bought into certain assumptions that may go unnoticed. A primary assumption can be the equating of the person[56] with the psychological personality[57]. If the person is the psychological personality, then the psychological interventions are treating the person. However, if one believes that there is both a person and a psychological personality, then a shift in thinking also needs to occur regarding treating the person. Psychological approaches would target psychological personality functioning[58], but what would target person functioning? One can consider this in terms of a verbal analogy.

Let me first explain what I mean by a verbal analogy. In a verbal analogy, one pair of related words has the same relationship as another word pair. When I was preparing to apply to graduate schools, I was required to take the Miller Analogies Test (MAT). The MAT is a high-level mental ability test requiring the solution of problems stated as analogies. The person taking the MAT is given pairs of related words along with other words without the other part of their pair. The examinee must find words that have the same relationship to the words that are in the first pair. For example: fire is to hot, as ice is to _____ would be answered by the word cold.

---

[56] **Person** is here defined as the immaterial aspect of the whole person (material and immaterial), and will here be considered as interchangeable with the terms soul, spirit, mind, and self − "whatever a person refers to when that person uses the term, 'I' to refer to himself or herself as a conscious agent" (Evans, *Separable souls: Dualism, selfhood, and the possibility of life after death*, 330).

[57] **Personality** refers to individual differences in characteristic patterns of thinking, feeling and behaving. The study of personality focuses on two broad areas: One is understanding individual differences in particular personality characteristics, such as sociability or irritability. The other is understanding how the various parts of a person come together as a whole. http://www.apa.org/topics/personality/

[58] **Personality Functioning** is the ability to achieve the whole person's goals within his or her self and the external environment. It includes an individual's behavior, emotion, social skills, and overall mental health. https://www.google.at/webhp?sourceid=chrome-instant&rlz=1C5CHFA_enUS556US560&ion=1&espv=2&ie=UTF-8#q=psycholog ical+functioning+definition

A verbal analogy can be made to compare the psychological personality and the person. If we were to start with the psychological personality, we could say that the psychological personality is to psychological functioning. What would we then put with the word person to form its pair? I believe that we would use the word character.[59] So in terms of the analogy, the psychological personality is to psychological functioning, as the person is to character. What have we then implied by this analogy?

I believe that the analogy clarifies that one cannot assume that psychological interventions will directly affect the person, rather psychological interventions that target psychological functioning are directly addressing a condition of the psychological personality. Likewise, interventions that are directly targeting the character (such as encouraging virtue formation through a relationship) are directly addressing a condition of the person. Now, what is more important to address, the personality or the person?

This may not be a fair question. If psychological problems are occurring, then naturally one must address the problem with psychological interventions. Under the assumption that the psychological personality is the person, one would believe that the person is also being helped directly. However, if one believes the psychological personality and the person are not the same, then the impact of the psychological intervention on the person is merely indirect − perhaps something about the therapeutic relationship was encouraging to the person or maybe the resolution of a psychological problem removed a barrier of dysfunction that was limiting the person. One can reasonably assume that the reverse is also true: improvements to the character of the person will have the indirect affect of improving the psychological functioning of the psychological personality.

---

[59] **Character** is the moral or ethical quality of the person and is the combination of virtues within the person that function together.

If one is talking about directly impacting the person, then is it really as significant as the outcome of impacting the psychological personality? Is the significance of the person at an equivalent level of importance to the significance of the psychological personality for improved personal functioning, in light of the challenges of life? I would say that although there is a correct analogy, there is not an equivalent level of significance. It seems self-evident that the psychological personality and functioning are not equivalent with the person and character. The functioning psychological personality is occurring within the human experience of the person. Therefore, the person is more significant. The person is to his psychological personality, as perhaps Tony Stark is to his Iron Man suit. (If you are not familiar with the Iron Man movie, there is a link below for an Iron Man [Suit Up] film clip.)[60] The super hero character, Tony Stark, built a suit that had certain capabilities, including a computer that Tony could interact with from within the suit. But make-no-mistake, Tony was the person animating the suit. When the illustration is understood this way, one can more clearly visualize the idea that the-person-is-not-the-same-as the brain and body. It is true, in the movie, that Tony and the suit are in some sense one, but they are also not one and the same. Tony and the suit become one, but Tony is always distinct from the suit and can always override what the suit and what its computer are doing, just as the person and personality are distinct. The person can override the personality. The person and the person's character, in a fundamental sense, are more significant than and different than the psychological personality and its psychological functioning.

Now back to the focus of the present material. The following material will elaborate on the relevance and importance of life mentoring's focus on virtues within the dynamic relationships between the life mentor and the client and God. The person, as more significant than the psychological personality, needs to be kept in mind. As well, the higher significance of focusing on the encouragement of the person's virtue development (character formation) than on the

---

60 Iron Man You Tube film clip: "Iron Man: Suit up", Cinema Stars Official, accessed September 5, 2016 https://www.youtube.com/watch?v=Fcm7OjoOz4A.

psychological personality's functioning needs to be maintained. In the life mentoring relationship, the encouragement of character is an important work — one that will impact the functioning of the whole person, including the psychological personality's functioning (see Appendix C for the challenge of modes). This following material is meant to improve life mentors' understanding of virtues and the formation of character.

The Virtue-in-Relationship Approach

The horizontal or person-to-person dynamic life mentoring relationship, replete with virtue modeling and exchanges, is intended to be a bridge to the enhancement of the quality of the client's dynamic moment by moment (real-time) relationship with God as life is happening. This virtue-in-relationships approach to spiritual development is also expected to result in client improvements in life management and flourishing. (See Appendix D for the important life mentor core conditions.)

In the life mentoring relationship, the client:

- Experiences the quality of character of the life mentor

- Learns about the needed virtues

- Is encouraged to be active in the development of character.

- Is moved toward a closer, real-time (here and now) relationship with God or improved utilization of the higher power.

The life mentor in relationship with clients:

- Listens as the clients tell their stories

- Does not deny the psychological and emotional issues and pain

- Chooses to help through the strengthening of character virtues

- Lives-out character virtues in life mentoring

- Points clients to the means of receiving grace from God or improved utilization of the higher power

- Encourages clients in practicing spiritual disciplines and virtues

- Refers clients for psychological help when it is needed.

Life mentoring is a different way of thinking about how to assist others. Virtues and relationship with God often operate in the background of life. What is more obvious are the problems in living and the focus on more concrete and common sense solutions that are action-oriented. If a person is depressed, for example, then the solution appears to be to directly change the depression. However, we know that a complete operational goal is not to merely reduce depression, because that is taking away a negative without replacing it with a positive. The obvious positive solution is to increase the person's joy in living, possibly through increased pleasurable activities and / or increasing positive interactions with others. What is missing even in this is the reality that it takes character qualities or virtues, as the foundation to these solutions, in order for the person to be able to practice or perform them. However, if instructed about the presence of and characteristics of virtues and the consequent actions connected to virtues, then clients become aware of and can be encouraged to identify virtues in their own internal lives that have always been operating, influencing emotional and relational living. The life mentoring strengthening of the soul, that results in enhanced personality functioning, is somewhat analogous to what physical therapy does in strengthening surrounding muscles, in order to compensate for an injured muscle and to prevent further loss of and promote improvement to functioning.

A Biblical Basis for Virtue-in-Relationship Influencing

One can inquire further about the validity of the idea that virtues influence emotional and relational living. For example, how does the virtue of love operate in and have an affect on relationships? There is immediate recognition, on the one hand, that loving versus unloving relationships are in sharp contrast. But, who generally identifies love as a virtue when thinking about a loving relationship. It is almost too obvious to recognize, but love is a virtue, not just a feeling or a decision. Love is, according to the Apostle Paul in Colossians 3:14, what binds everything together in perfect harmony. He says this in the context of having listed the virtues that are to be "put on:" compassionate hearts, kindness, humility, meekness, and patience. These appear to be at least some of the virtues that the meta-virtue of love binds together. The cluster of virtues that loves binds together are immensely and self-evidently beneficial for relationships. Likewise, the Apostle Peter also writes that virtues need to be increasing (2 Peter 1:5) and that they are linked together with brotherly affection and love.

The virtue of love is biblically indicated as having huge consequences relationally with God and others (1 John 4:7-12). Anyone who does not love does not know God. By contrast, whoever loves has been born of God and knows God. What can be more evident of the relational significance of the virtue of love than the statement by the Apostle John that if we love one another, God abides in us and his love is perfected in us.

One might say that Christians are commanded to love one another. That is true, but the mere statement of this truth is not clarifying of the connection between the inner virtue of love and the outward action of love. It is out of the heart that the actions flow, and this can be understood as the flowing-out of virtues from deep within the person. Good is produced out of the virtue treasures that these persons have in their hearts (Luke 6:45). They are righteous persons, but not in the sense of saving Righteousness. Rather, they are righteous/virtuous in the sense of consequent or resulting righteousness — the righteousness that flows out a life made new and having the Righteousness of Christ.

A new person, a regenerated person has been imputed with the Righteousness of Christ for salvation and has renewed virtues. Into the regenerated person's life comes experiences, even of suffering, that are part of the process of further character development. God is in this process with the person and his love is poured-out into the person's heart (Romans 5:3-5). The resulting righteousness is the goodness of character virtues flowing out of the heart, creating a righteous, sincere, and good love toward others. Christ's Righteousness is complete and perfect, but this righteousness-as-virtues-in-the-heart is not initially complete or perfect. It must be increasing in completeness and perfection throughout life.

Quality of Love Virtue for Quality of Real-Time Relationship with God

Perhaps if one were asked to identify what virtue most closely exemplifies righteous, the virtue of love would suffice. After all, the one who loves another has fulfilled the law (Romans 13:8). The quality of ones love is related to the quality of relationships, including ones real-time relationship with God.

One could say that the primary focus in life mentoring is on the virtue of love, because the quality of the client's virtue of love is critical for the quality of the client's character and the quality of the client's real-time relationship with God. The "quality of the client's character" refers to the virtues present in the client and how well-developed and practically applied those virtues are for daily living. In other words, the client's ability to function and flourish in life, amid it's many challenges is directly associated with how developed and operational are the virtues held within the person and from the person toward others. Virtues are directly connected with personal functioning and flourishing in life. To live with underdeveloped character, by contrast, is to not have character virtues as an established resource to engage with life and to be more fully and positively present in relationships.

What is meant by the phrase, "the quality of the client's real-time relationship with God?" Real-time relationship refers to the how well clients are able to, in the here and now, connect with the loving presence of God in the activities of the outward life and in the processes of the inward life. To have a real-time relationship with God is to have a dynamic loving relationship with God as life is lived. This dynamic (active, changing, responsive, and progressing[61]) loving relationship is the immediate involvement and interaction of God with the person. The stronger the person's virtues are, particularly the virtue of love, the more deeply and strongly intimate will be the connection in real-time relating.

As the virtue of love increases, clients are more able to hold the reality of God's existing in the present time and being actively engaged with them, even though God is invisible and not heard as an audible voice. This type of connection with God should not be too much to imagine for the person who has the ability to hold internal representations of loved ones, even while apart from these loved ones. The connection with the loved one is "experienced" even though not physically present. The person has the ability to bring the physically absent loved one into current situations and internal processes in a relationally dynamic manner. The client should, in other words, be able to believe and trust intellectually and emotionally that the loved ones affection, commitment, understanding, and other dimensions of relationship are really present. With God there is an added reality to this type

---

[61] Please do not misunderstand this comment to be saying that God is changing or evolving in response to us. God's essence is unchanging.

of connection, because unlike the absent loved one, God is really present everywhere, at all times, and to the same extent, and He is responsive.

When considering this immediate and constant experiencing of relationship with God, questions may arise about whether God relates in real-time. However, this intimate way of God relating with people is biblically documented in Jesus' interactions with people. There are recorded accounts of actual person-to-person interactions that Jesus had with individuals (e.g., with the Samaritan woman at the well, the woman caught in the act of adultery, or Peter in the reinstatement after betraying Jesus). In life mentoring, the client is encouraged to be open to God's personal, powerful, good, and loving relating in the here and now. The client's necessary personal condition, for receiving and resonating with a real-time relationship with the Lord, is a progressively growing quality of character. Virtues consistent with the character of God are necessary for a fuller and deeper intimacy in ones relationship with God. In other words, the more similarity in character with Christ, the more this real-time relationship will flourish.

The Connection Between Virtue and Truth

The quality of ones character seems like an easy thing to identify based on relationship interactions with the person over time. We would be able to tell from these interactions how the person responds and whether the person responds in a manner that is virtuous. But, how does one determine both what the desirable virtues are and how these virtues are to be correctly defined. To do this defining requires a trusted reference for finding the content. One can look to psychological research and anthropological sources in an attempt to define what healthy virtuousness would look like. One can explore cross-culturally for the virtues that appear to transcend cultures and are in common. Attempts can be made to derive consistent definitions for the virtues. These attempts would provide some basis for speaking about more universally desirable virtues. However, this approach is only partially satisfying for individuals who reference the Bible as the ultimate authoritative source of moral knowledge.

The Bible provides an authoritative and ultimate reference for those who trust in its validity and reliability. God is trusted as the ultimate author of the Bible, who has guaranteed the Bible's truthfulness. The Bible is then believed to provide the content for knowing virtues and virtuousness. Well-researched and thought-out biblical and theological interpretations of the virtues would further be trusted to provide accurate definitions for virtues. Knowledge of Christ, as revealed in the Gospels and elsewhere in the Bible, would be a rich source to determine what the virtues look like in action, including interpersonal relatedness.

Biblical truth provides the content for understanding virtues and the desired character quality of individuals who are virtuous or righteous. In this regard, virtue and truth are inseparably connected. Though regarding virtues as truth may sound like an impersonal perspective, the nature of truth takes on a personalness when thought of as existing within the person of Christ, as definite virtues and a consistent quality of character. Christians are to move in the direction of a quality of character that is more completely and fully Christ-like. The Bible, when understood as a book that is its own commentary, lists and defines the virtues that are truly the quality character of Christ and Christlikeness.

A Further Look at Virtue-Based Change[62]

The growth in the quality of character, in a Christian, can be thought of as a sanctification and spiritual transformation process. There can be confusion, however, about what is meant by sanctification and spiritual transformation. Both terms are used to refer to change. To reduce the confusion and add clarity in our

---

[62]   Morgan, *Fighting for Peace*. Chapter 11.

discussion of change, *sanctification* and *spiritual transformation* are here being used as equivalent and interchangeable. If fact, Christian spiritual transformation must be seen as the same thing as sanctification — the same process. If it is something partially or all together different, then what is spiritual transformation and where is it taking the person? The goal is always rightly to be transformed into the likeness of Christ.

When thinking of virtues changing within a person, we should not confuse self-improvement or improvements that come from person-to-person connections, with the sanctifying work of the Holy Spirit. Sanctification is dependent on God. The Holy Spirit activates in the person the truth that transforms — the truth that is the transformation of virtue within the person toward more consistency with Christ. (One might say that Christ is truth embodied — John 1:1-5, John 5:39-40.) However, there are numerous helpful self-improvement practices that can be useful in our cooperating in the sanctification process, including practicing spiritual disciplines (such as solitude, silence, fasting, serving others, confession) and being involved in transformation promoting relationships. However, the Holy Spirit illuminating truth in our hearts is the actual means for becoming Christ-like in our character. These are helpful practices that can be useful in the process of preparing ourselves for sanctification, including practicing spiritual disciplines and being involved in life mentoring and other encouraging relationships. Additionally, truth as applied by the Spirit — illuminated in the person's heart by the Spirit — is the real means for transformation. This sanctifying work alters beliefs and establishes virtues in the heart of the person.[63]

The Holy Spirit is actively present and the person is participating. Human relationships intersect with spiritual transformation by encouraging the application of virtue related biblical truth to the heart and actions of another. Beyond that application by human words or deeds, the Holy Spirit supernaturally works within the person. The sanctifying work of the Holy Spirit and being

---

[63] Young, *Reinventing Your Life*, 14-18. and Crabb, *Inside Out*, 81.

sanctified with the truth can be understood as meaning that the type and quality of ones virtues are becoming more consistent with those of Christ.

When desiring to grow in a Christian virtue, such as humility, we can identify our need and how we go wrong with our pride (the vice opposite to humility). We can set our goal to be more humble. We can then further understand psychological hindrances such as faulty beliefs. Spiritual disciplines can be practiced and the means of grace such as prayer and reading of scripture, but the human side of these attempts to change are not sufficient. This brings us to the ultimate source of change: God Himself. The Apostle Paul fully understood his own struggle with spiritual transformation (see Romans Chapter 7). However, Paul understood not only *what* needs to change but also *how* to change or more accurately *who* changes us most deeply – the Holy Spirit doing his sanctifying work. The Holy Spirit is God the Counselor, indwelling and working change in us. Paul understood how change was really taking place in his life. Paul acknowledged transformation as ultimately being supernatural and centered on the One whom He wanted to know.

In Philippians chapter 3, the Apostle Paul revealed to us his deep desire to know Jesus. This knowing Jesus cannot be overlooked in discussions of, explanations for, and practices toward spiritual transformation. Jesus is alive and He is Lord over everything, including our change. Paul said that he counted "...everything as loss because of the surpassing worth of knowing Christ Jesus my Lord." (Philippians 3:8) Paul wanted to "be found in him [Jesus], not having a righteousness of my own that comes from the law, but that which comes through faith in Christ..." (Philippians 3:9) Paul went on, in this biblical context, to reveal his one primary, essential, transformational focus in his Christian life – "that I may know him [Jesus] and the power of his resurrection, and may share in his sufferings, becoming like him in his death." (Philippians 3:10) This is virtue transformation in relationship.

Knowing Jesus relationally is transforming. Knowing Jesus is not neutral, but includes being changed. This knowing is not just an intellectual understanding, but also knowing in a personal way. This "knowing" Jesus is available every moment of our Christian lives. We are never outside this real-time (here and now) relationship. However, for various reasons we may ignore, resist, lack comprehension of, have difficulty trusting and generally misunderstand the significant reality of Jesus' affect on us and the working of the Holy Spirit in us.

If Paul's example is followed, our love for, our desire for Jesus is so real that all other things in this life are by comparison rubbish. All other things do not stand up to "the surpassing worth of knowing Christ Jesus my Lord." (Philippians 3:8) We may try many means to change, but if these means are ever divorced from or practiced separate from an acknowledgement of the surpassing worth of knowing Christ, then these means are rubbish[64].

One may still wonder how being in relationship with Jesus brings about our change. Change is here to be understood as righteousness or virtues or Christ-like character being formed in us. Paul in Philippians 3:21 states that it is Jesus who ultimately "will transform our lowly bodies to be like his glorious body..."[65] This transforming is sanctification or spiritual transformation by being transformed to have the virtues of Jesus integrated into ones character and the opposing vices diminished.

---

[64] *Spirit of the Reformation Study Bible,* 2158. The Belgic Confession, in Article 21 states the following. "Therefore we rightly say with Paul that we 'know nothing but Jesus and him crucified'; we consider all things as 'dung for the excellence of the knowledge of our Lord Jesus Christ.' We find all comforts in his wounds and have no need to seek or invent any other means to reconcile ourselves with God than this one and only sacrifice, once made, which renders believers perfect forever."

[65] Ferguson, *The Holy* Spirit, 170. "Calvin refers to this aspect of the Spirit's work in bringing communion as well as union with Christ as a duplex, or two-fold, mortification (*mortificatio*) and vivification (*vivificatio*). Internally, sanctification involves death to sin, rejection of sin, and consecration to God in new life; externally (since sanctification touches our whole being), it involves the mortification of bearing the cross in all manner of afflictions and persecutions, and ultimately the vivification of the resurrection."

Paul provides further understanding when he states that he wants to know Christ and "the power of his resurrection" and "share his sufferings." (Philippians 3:10) These two factors of power and suffering are operating in the change-imparting relationship with Jesus. The power of his resurrection is his power over sin and death as well as his sinless life being manifested in us as we live with him. In the fellowship of his suffering every bit of our suffering is used by Jesus to transform us.[66]

> *For the righteous will never be moved; he will be remembered forever. He is not afraid of bad news; his heart is firm, trusting in the LORD.* Ps. 112:6-7

Summary Points

Life Mentoring Virtues to Develop Character:

1. Virtues are understood to reside within the soul, who is the real person, though being expressed through the rest of the person (brain and body).

2. Virtues are believed to be present in all people as a part of the image of God.

3. Virtues can grow and the potential for growth is greater for Christians, whose souls have been regenerated, freed from the power of sin, and who have the Holy Spirit's illuminating and strengthening at work within them.

---

[66] *Spirit of the Reformation Study* Bible, 2180. The Westminster Confession of Faith Chapter 13 states the following. "2. This sanctification is throughout the whole man; yet imperfect in this life, there abiding still some remnants of corruption in every part, whence ariseth a continual and irreconcilable war, the flesh lusting against the Spirit, and the Spirit against the flesh. 3. In which war, although the remaining corruption, for a time, may much prevail; yet through the continual supply of strength from the sanctifying Spirit of Christ, the regenerate part doth overcome; and so, the saints grow in grace, perfecting holiness in the fear of God."

The Life Mentoring Structured and Supervised Practice

Introduction to the Structured Practice

Though the structured practice may seem to be all about the *Life in Process* material, it is not. The material is merely like a friendly computer program interface. You become the life mentoring, as the stages of change and the principles integrate into who you are and as you continue on in your own process of: growing self-awareness, relating with God intimately, and cooperating with Holy Spirit in your virtue-related character formation.

Life mentoring is not a new idea or a unique technique. It just provides one description of and illumination of the personal growth and sanctifying process already at work. Life mentoring is an attempt to give a human understanding to a heavenly truth. You are not being asked to become some kind of guru or wise sage, just a person who has learned more about the process of change and has allowed that process to become reflexive and intentional both personally and interpersonally.

The *Life in Process* practice material is structured into a series of selected worksheets (one worksheet per session), so that it will carry itself as you go through it with your client. You'll chose a client who is strong enough and willing enough to go through the practice with you − even with your likely, at times, awkwardness and imperfection. Your presence in the process is most important and change will happen even in spite of your imperfections. Of course, that's no excuse for you not trying your best, and I believe you will. This training process invites mistakes and embraces them − you try, we review, make adjustments, and you try again. Doing the structured practice well is putting yourself out there, being willing to look honestly at how you are doing, and receiving feedback and modify along the way.

In helping others change, whether in a teaching context or mentoring/counseling context, a one-size approach isn't possible. So, there have to be adjustments to make the process fit individual readiness. We will need to decide the post-training that you are ready for and want.

There are different ways to go about the post phase of the life mentor training, and it can be altered to fit. The material presented here is for individuals who are ready or will soon be a ready to do the life mentoring supervised practice.

Boundaries in Life Mentor Practice

A boundary is a border or limit. It may be the farthest limit or a marked area. In life mentoring, as in counseling, the term "boundaries" is used to define the emotional and physical space that we place between oneself and others. Setting proper boundaries is important for our mental and spiritual health, as well as for appropriately assisting others by maintaining boundaries in helping.

Boundaries are learned in early relationships, especially in families. The extent to which a person automatically has appropriate emotional and physical boundaries, in relationships, is to a large extend explained by the boundary quality of those early relationships. As well, faulty boundary setting and maintaining has its origins in early relationships, combined with the remaining effects of fallenness. An improving character / virtue development, along with an increasing understanding of and effectiveness in boundary setting, will not only help the life mentor to personally function well, but will also have a positive relationship impact on clients.

Compassion is a virtue in the Christian life and very important for the life mentoring relationship, as long as the compassion stays within appropriate emotional and physical boundaries. Compassion Fatigue (CF) refers to the taking-in or taking-on of another person's problems, as ones own to feel and to be responsible for. Helper compassion fatigue is also known as secondary traumatization or secondary post-traumatic stress disorder, which is equivalent to PTSD.[67]

---

[67] Simpson & Starkey, *Secondary traumatic stress, compassion fatigue and counselor spirituality: Implications for counselors working with trauma.*

Compassion Fatigue is a state of exhaustion and dysfunction – biologically, psychologically, and socially. A common theme, in the research, is that work that is focused on the relief of clients' emotional suffering typically results in the helper's absorption of information about human suffering, which is stressful. Individuals differ and some are more able to tolerate exposure to stressors without negative manifestations, while others are not.

An explanation of differing abilities to manage the stress relates to the effectiveness in maintaining boundaries. Boundaries serve as a filtering system and are foundational to use in coping with the stress that comes with helping others. Also differences in the presence and use of coping techniques to handle stressors are related to the impact of compassion fatigue. Research indicates helper well-being contributes to avoidance of compassion fatigue symptoms. Religion and spirituality (as a personally meaningful experience) were found to have a positive correlation with immunity to stressful situations.[68]

Other areas of boundary maintaining in life mentoring have to do with competence, and confidentiality. **Competence** means limiting helping to the areas in which one has knowledge, training, and experience. In life mentoring, this means that the trained life mentor can provide a certain kind of help. The goals that a life mentor sets with a client need to match the type of helping competence of the life mentor. Life mentors are assisting clients with managing personal issues by deepening their real-time relationship with God and by growing in related virtues. The boundary of competence or limit would, for example, stop before moving into practicing counseling with its related types of goals that extend more deeply into psychological functioning.

Boundaries are also a way of describing the decisions and actions that limit the use of personal information given to life mentors by the clients. This is the issue of **confidentiality**. Certain

---

[68]   Ibid.

professions are mandated to keep client information confidential and not release the information without client consent or by legal requirement. Life mentors do not come under these laws, but nonetheless need to guard what client information is released and to whom. Clients need to be informed that their information, from the life mentoring practice meetings, will be shared with the supervisor, for the purpose of the life mentor's training.

Another issue related to life mentoring and boundaries has to do with whether to do life mentoring with someone with whom there could be a **physical attraction**. There may appear to be a simple answer: don't do it! However, that does not adequately take into consideration the level of vulnerability of either or both people in the mentoring relationship. This would be a concern if, for example, either person is currently in a problematic romantic relationship that could leave the person vulnerable to the attention / even caring of a person with whom there could be an attraction. By contrast, a significant age difference between the life mentor and the client would likely mean a lower risk of boundary crossing. However, a general rule of only doing life mentoring with individuals with whom there is not the potential for sexual attraction would be the safest, and probably wisest, policy.

Supervision will be helpful in identifying boundaries in life mentoring – when they are working well and when they are being crossed. This is an opportunity to discuss why boundary crossing happens, and how to re-establish and better maintain appropriate and healthy boundaries in life mentoring.

The setting and maintaining of boundaries in life mentoring reflects the functioning and flourishing of the life mentor. When boundaries are operating well in a person, then there is evidence of the virtue of self-control – an ability to stay within the limits of the particular situation, with a particular person with whom there is a certain type of relationship. A positive byproduct of knowing the boundaries is a greater sense of peace and confidence that comes from knowing how, how much, and in what manner to help.

Stages Within Each Life Mentoring Meeting

In the Life Mentor Training, descriptions are provided for the stages of change in the overall process of life mentoring. These stages are connected with the chapter content in the book *Life in Process* and its worksheets. The *Life in Process* chapter content is utilized to enhance the teaching of the stages (see Appendix E: Stages of Change), and the worksheets provide a structure to focus on both life goals and situational goals. The content in *Life in Process* corresponds well with the overall stages in the whole life mentoring set of meetings. The practice set of meetings follows selected chapter content, such that the life mentoring practice is divided into a series of meetings that the life-mentor-in-training goes through with a client. Meetings cover the *Life in Process* chapter content, by use of related worksheets (see Worksheet Examples in Appendix F).

The training, with its practice, has been designed to be a simplified way to grasp the repeating pattern of stages (beginning, middle, and end) that is an effective way to assist another person through challenging issues and toward better coping. In life mentoring, the process in the stages is also used to increase intimacy in ones relationship with God and growth in character – virtue development.

In the training, mention is made of the fact that all helping does not go in a linear manner from beginning to end. Clients may have already been thinking about themselves in their challenging situation and may have even defined situational goals, and perhaps even tried to take action on those goals. As well, clients likely have more than one issue in life that triggers, for example, unmanageableness. In real life helping, the life mentor needs to be able to identify the stage that the person is in with an issue, in order to enter into the process to assist in bringing about change.

There are two levels of stages, the overall process across all the meetings goes through the three stages, and the three stages are happening within each meeting as related to the client's ongoing disclosed story. The three-stage process happens in each meeting with a client and perhaps repeats more than once in the same meeting, as the client talks about personal issues. One image of the repeating stages is a Russian Nesting Doll. Within each doll is another similar doll. Using this image, one can consider that within the overall stages, across all the meetings, are similar smaller occurrences of the stages in each meeting.

To illustrate this, let's consider the Life Mentoring structured practice worksheets. The life mentor is to lead the client through a worksheet for each meeting. The following stages are also repeated in each meeting:[69]

1. *Telling Their Story* – **Current Picture**

2. *Setting Situational Goals* – **The Preferred Picture**

3. *Taking Action* – **The Way Forward**

The material in each chapter (with its worksheet) can be understood as relating to these stages. The worksheets are all designed to contain the following parts: Summary Points, Processing Questions, and Characteristic God Responses. There is a natural connection between these worksheet parts and working the stages.

Correspondence of Within Meeting Stages and the Worksheet

The three stages can be applied to each meeting by starting with the **Current Picture** stage. In this stage, you are helping clients tell their story. You give information in the Summary Points, Processing Questions, and Characteristic God Responses sections of the worksheets. As you give that information, you are allowing clients to react. Of course you are structuring their comments to the content of that worksheet and not letting them tell their

---

[69] Egan, *The skilled helper: A Problem-Management and Opportunity-Development Approach to Helping.*

story more generally, but you are still getting their thoughts, ideas, feelings and struggles. By going over these points in the worksheet, for a particular topic (e.g., the worksheet topic of Unmanageableness — see Appendix F), you are helping clients tell their stories.

Regarding **The Preferred Picture**, the correspondence needs some clarification. For this worksheet, the content related to the within meeting stages is focused on identifying unmanageableness. In other words, this worksheet topic explores what needs to be more managed, and in the meeting you help the client begin to define and translate their story of unmanageableness into viable situational goals.[70] These are the situational goals that come from the content of clients' stories and are according to their desires.

Clients might state some things ("goals") they have already identified as important to be moving toward in light of their identified unmanageableness. You can encourage the clarifying those within meeting goals, or if clients do not have a goal direction, you can help identify goals from what they have disclosed and connected them to the general topic of that chapter's worksheet. The meeting situational goals should also be connected to clients' life goals: the here-and-now relationship with God and virtue formation. A commonly needed virtue / character quality in the unmanageableness worksheet would be the quality of self-awareness.

For example, after the clients have commented on their reaction to the Summary Points, Processing Questions, and Characteristic God Responses sections, you can ask what they would like to see happening in their own life — their desires. For instance, if a young man has told you that his unmanageableness is about being anxious about his work, then you can ask how he would like to feel about his work and how he would like to believe God is with him in his anxiousness about work. These are situational and life related goals from within the meeting.

---

[70] Please see Appendix G for clarifications regarding the simultaneous use of both *life goals* and *situational goals*.

The final stage that needs to happen in the meeting is **The Way Forward**. This involves helping clients make some decisions about what to do, in other words, helping clients develop strategies and actions to accomplish meeting goals. It should be fairly obvious what clients have been doing that isn't working, but they need to tell what they have tried that does provide some success too.

Remember, if you jump to telling clients what they need to do before they have more fully told their story (as you've assisted them through the worksheet) or before they have stated what they want (goals as you have helped them to clarify from their reactions to the worksheet), then you are likely slipping into advice giving, fixing, and taking inappropriate responsibility (a form of control). The decision about what clients need to do should flow naturally from the work done in the meeting, as shaped and influenced also by you. Also, please keep in mind the life goals – that whatever action is to be taken should be connected with God's characteristic response to his children. As well, the action should reflect a virtue or character quality that needs to be present that will counter the negative reaction to the unmanageableness that has previously been happening (see Appendix E). For example, going from being unaware of oneself, toward more awareness.

Final Comments on the Structured Practice

Though this process of stages may all seem far too complex, it will get better with practice. The analogy of learning how to drive a car is an appropriate comparison with learning how to do life mentoring. At first, there are so many things to do and to be aware of at the same time that it seems impossible to even remember, let alone coordinate them smoothly. However, if I know each thing well, I have already made progress toward driving. If I do not know the "things" that have to be done, then my driving will be like a friend of mine, who for the first time behind the wheel in drivers training class took off smoothly and promptly tried to shift from first gear to reverse! He later admitted to having no knowledge of the shift pattern – an unfortunate incident for the car and an unfortunate lapse in my friend's character, for he had indicated to the instructor that he knew what he was doing.

The supervised practice time in the life mentor training is a perfect opportunity to jettison any need to appear competent and to embrace the grace that will be extended in the learning process. Unlike a content-oriented course in school, there is no way to have all the answers ahead of time in order to perfectly pass the test. We are all "practicing" every time we get behind the "wheel" of helping another person. Lets be as informed as possible and as humble as befitting the complex task of entering into another person's world for the purpose of influencing positively

Final Thoughts on Life Mentor Training

Warning about Training in and the Practice of Counseling

Counseling is a profession. After my years of full-time teaching in both counseling graduate school programs and in a seminary pastoral counseling program, I have an informed perspective on the training of counselors. Here's one of my views: Counseling should be done by academically trained, supervised, and licensed professionals. Certifications in counseling, counseling training in non-clinical academic programs, and non-university based training in counseling are not preparation for the profession of counseling. It is ignorance and/or deception to promote these "counseling programs" as leading to the person being a trained professional counselor.

I don't offer this criticism only because of a personal bias. In the US, there is a movement toward a tightening-up on the standards for the professional training of counselors. There have been, for some time, rigorous state licensing requirements for counselors (and even higher level training requirements for psychologists). In recent years a national accreditation has been gaining influence and authority, CACREP. CACREP is the standard that training programs now aspire to, and their accreditation will likely become the standard for the counseling profession (in psychology it is accreditation by the American Psychological Association). Any individual or organization that promotes itself as training counselors, but is not located in an academic institution, does not follow state licensure requirements, and does not conform to CACREP standards, is suspect and should not be trusted as offering viable training in the profession of counseling. Further, to call oneself a "counselor," but to not be professionally trained is a misrepresentation and constitutes a risk to the clients being helped.

What I have just stated may sound like harsh criticisms and/or as a capitulation to the secular world. I would suggest that it is arrogant for the Christian community to believe that because of having God's truth in the Bible, that they therefore have the rightful authority to train and practice in a variety of disciplines, including counseling. Perhaps it is my thirty-plus years of witnessing ignorant and arrogant attitudes within the Christian community regarding counseling and psychology that has lead me to be so blunt. All truth is God's truth, whether found in special revelation or discovered in creation. If we are humble and honest, we can admit that the secular world is also a vehicle through which God reveals the truth in His creation. Respect should be paid to the people and organizations that have devoted themselves to discovery and development in the field of professional counseling. The professional Christian counseling community and Christian professional counseling training programs, with their qualified faculty, are able to discern, shape, and conform the secular knowledge gained to be compatible with a biblical world and life view.

Appropriate Ways to Help Others

The negative statements in the prior section should not be taken as an attempt to territorially limit or prevent non-professional people from helping others. Christians in particular should not feel offended just because they are told that unless they are professionally trained, they cannot "counsel" others in need. The title Counselor has a specific meaning in the field of professional counseling. Let's reserve that title for the people who are appropriately trained and licensed. Let us also not promote confusion about or a misrepresentation of the type of assistance that non-professionally trained and non-licensed helpers are providing.

There are ways for lay helpers and especially ways for Christians to come along side of others in a supportive, healing, and growth-oriented manner. But this is not, nor does it need to be called counseling. There must be a matching of training, focus, and goals with the service being offered, in order for the way of helping others to be appropriate. Professional counselors are trained in rigorous programs, they appropriately focus on the psychological processes, and they set goals that will lead to the accomplishment of psychological healing and growth.

By contrast, other helpers must look to their own training, their focus in the one being helped, and the related goals in order to appropriately assist the other person. Any Christian is within the limits of appropriateness to offer certain kinds of assistance to others. For example, if a Christian has mechanical skills, then someone who is having a mechanical problem that fits with the Christian's skill set will benefit from the Christian figuring-out the mechanical problem and pursuing the solution. Further, a Christian is always within the confines of appropriateness to offer to pray for the needs of another person who is receptive (given that the prayer itself is sensitive and conforms to biblical truth). If a Christian has other life and career skills, then assistance can be offered, but not as counseling. A more general and non-counseling term, such as discipling or mentoring can be used, if a name for the help is even necessary. The main point here is to not fall into or deliberately move into a helping focus and goal setting that is outside ones own competence.

The Life Mentor Training Alternative

Life mentoring training is purposefully designed to carefully avoid preparing people to believe that they are becoming "counselors." Instead, life mentoring presents a non-counseling paradigm for helping. The paradigm for training and helping does not directly focus on the psychological aspects of the person, and the goals are not to directly accomplish counseling related healing and growth. Because of this, life mentoring steers away from counseling and toward an appropriate spiritual focus with spiritual growth goals. Whatever improved psychological functioning that results is because of the overall spiritual gains that make the person more able to cope and have more resilience with regard to life challenges.

Counseling is just one of many ways to assist, as medicine or dentistry are ways of assisting. Each has its own professional standards of training, focused areas of treatment competence, and procedures for attaining treatment goals. Professionals in each area of competence know that they need to stay within their disciple when practicing. As well, life mentoring has a defined training, a focused area of competence, and ways to bring about the goals for change.

Life mentoring is not a newly created helping profession designed to replace counseling. However, the "knife" cuts both ways. Professionally trained and licensed counselors, with only clinical counseling training, should not attempt to do life mentoring, as it is here defined. Life mentoring is here defined as a particular approach to helping, with its focus primarily on the soul-person and the person's relationship with God. The goals are connected to both character development and deepened here-and-now personal relatedness with God. Life mentoring can be a compliment to work being done in counseling, just as counseling can be a compliment to work being done by the client with a life mentor. Life mentoring and counseling have differing goals that are congruent with a differing focus. Life mentoring focuses directly on the person and character, and counseling focuses on the personality and it's functioning.

Life mentoring is a real way to help others that the profession of counseling itself is not prepared to do. It is a rigorously designed training that has been developed over decades, by a person who has significant relevant academic and professional credentials and experience. Hopefully, *An Introduction to Life Mentor Training* has sharpened your understanding of what life mentoring is and how it is a distinct way of preparation in order to assist others. Though it is possible to help others and to be used by God without being well-trained, please consider the advantages both personally and for the sake of others that are derived from having invested in an organized training over a reasonably lengthy time of preparation.

Hopefully by this point enough information has been provided to offer a clear picture of the Life Mentor Training and its helpful benefits. In case there remains some lack of clarity, these final thoughts are offered. Your specific reactions and questions are also welcomed.

Summary Points

Life Mentoring Summarized:

1. Life mentoring addresses the soul and the functioning of the soul's character virtues, by providing a real relationship that models a healthy caring relationship and demonstrates Christ-like virtues.

2. The expectation is that sinful dispositions in the brain (and rest of the body) will weaken, as the soul's virtues are strengthened and real-time relating with God improves.

3. Through the experience and practice of character virtues and real-time reliance on God, it is expected that eventually problems with personality functioning will be more contained and better managed.

References

References

Arntz, Arnoud and Gitta Jacob. *Schema Therapy In Practice: An Introductory Guide to the Schema Mode Approach.* Chichester, UK: Wiley –Blackwell, 2013

Beauregard, Mario & O'Leary, Denyse. *The Spiritual Brain: A Neuroscientist's Case for the Existence of the Soul.* New York: HarperCollins, 2007.

Beck, James R and Bruce A Demarest. *The Human Person In Theology And Psychology.* Grand Rapids, MI: Kregel, 2005.

Berkhof, Lewis. *Systematic Theology.* Grand Rapids: MI: Wm B. Eerdmans, 1993.

Berkhof, Louis. *A Summary Of Christian Doctrine.* Carlisle, PA: Banner of Truth Trust, 1960.

Berkouwer, Gerrit Cornelis. *Man: The image of God.* Grand Rapids: Eerdmans, 1962.

Brugger, Christian & The Faculty of the Institute for the Psychological Sciences. "Anthropological foundations for clinical psychology: A proposal" *Journal of Psychology and Theology,* 36, (2008): 3-15.

Calvin, John. *Genesis.* Calvin's Commentaries. 22 vols. Grand Rapids: Baker Book House, 1996

Cooper, John W. *Body, Soul, And Life Everlasting.* Grand Rapids, Mich.: Eerdmans, 2000.

Crabb, Larry. *Inside Out.* Colorado Springs, Colo.: NavPress, 1988.

Douglas, James Dixon, ed. *The New Bible Dictionary.* Grand Rapids: Eerdmans, 1977.

Egan, Gerard. *The skilled helper: A Problem-Management and Opportunity-Development Approach to Helping* (8th ed.). Pacific Grove, CA: Brooks/Cole Publishing, 2007.

Evans, C. Stephen. "Separable souls: Dualism, selfhood, and the possibility of life after death". *Christian Scholar's Review, 34*, (2005) 327-340.

Ferguson, Sinclair. *The Holy Spirit.* Downers Grove, IL: InterVarsity Press, 1996.

Gangel, Kenneth. *Communication and Conflict Management in Churches and Christian Organizations.* Nashville: Broadman & Holeman, 1992.

Gelso, Charles J. "Emerging and Continuing Trends in Psychotherapy: Views From an Editor's Eye". *Psychotherapy,* Vol. 48, No. 2, (2011), 182–187

George, Timothy. *Galatians.* The New American Commentary; Nashville: Broadman & Holman, 1994.

Girardeau, John. *Discussions of Theological Questions.* Harrisonburg, VA: Sprinkle Publications, 1986.

Goetz, Steward & Taliaferro, Charles. *A Brief History of the Soul.* West Sussex, UK: Wiley-Blackwell, 2011.

Grudem, Wayne. *Systematic Theology: An Introduction to Biblical Doctrine.* Grand Rapids, MI: Zondervan, 1994.

Johnson, Eric. "Describing the Self within Redemptive History". *Journal of Psychology and Christianity*, 19, (2000), 5-24.

Kirschenbaum, Howard & Jourdan, April. "The Current Status of Carl Rogers and The Person-Centered Approach". *Psychotherapy: Theory, Research, Practice, Training.* 42 (1), (2005), 37-51.

Ladd, George Eldon. *A Theology of the New Testament.* Grand Rapids: Wm. B. Eerdmans Publishing Co, 1993.

Morgan, Dennis. *The Soul That Suffers: A Perspective on Human Nature and Suffering for Counseling Christians.* Chesapeake, VA: Watertree Press, 2013.

Morgan, Dennis. "Soul as the person experiencing the brain's psychological functioning". *Edification Journal.* 5(1), (2011), 45-53.

Morgan, Dennis. *Fighting for Peace: Combating conflict with character.* Chesapeake, VA: Watertree Press, 2009.

Morgan, Dennis. *Life in Process.* Wheaton, IL: Victor Books, 1993.

Mounce, Robert H. *Romans.* The New American Commentary. Vol. 27. Nashville: Broadman & Holman, 1995.

Murray, John. "The Epistle to the Romans (vol. 1)". in *The new international commentary,* ed. Bruce, Frederick Fyvie. Grand Rapids, MI: Wm. B. Eerdmans, 1971.

Nagel, Thomas. "What is it Like to be a Bat?" In Block, Ned. *Readings in Philosophy of Psychology.* Vol. 1. Cambridge, MA: Harvard University Press, 1980.

Reymond, Robert. *A New Systematic Theology of the Christian Faith.* Nashville, TN: Thomas Nelson, 1998.

Robinson, Daniel N. *An Intellectual History of Psychology.* Madison, WI: The University of Wisconsin Press, 1986.

Schwartz, Jeffery and Madden, Rebecca. *You Are Not Your Brain: The 4-Step Solution for Changing Bad Habits, Ending Unhealthy Thinking, and Taking Control of Your Life.* New York: Avery, 2011

Seligman, Martin. *Authentic Happiness*. New York: Free Press, 2002.

Shepherd, Katherine, Coifman, Karin, Matt, Lindsey, & Fresco, David. "Development of a Self-Distancing Task and Initial Validation of Responses". *Psychological Assessment*. 28(7), (2016), 841-855.

Simpson, Laura R. and Starkey, Donna S. "Secondary Traumatic Stress, Compassion Fatigue And Counselor Spirituality: Implications For Counselors Working With Trauma". *Counselingoutfitters. com*, 2006. http://counselingoutfitters.com/Simpson.htm.

Spirit of the Reformation Study Bible. Grand Rapids, MI: Zondervan, 2003.

Stott, John. *Men Made New*. Downers Grove, IL: InterVarsity Press, 1970.

Verduyn, Philippe; Van Mechelen, Iven; Kross, Ethan. "The Relationship Between Self-Distancing and the Duration of Negative and Positive Emotional Experiences in Daily Life". Emotion. Vol. 12 (6),(2012), 1248–1263.

Westminster Confession of Faith. Glasgow, Scotland: Free Presbyterian Publications, 2003.

Young, Jeffery. *Reinventing Your Life*. New York: Plume, Penguin Books, 1994

Appendices

Appendix A: Life Mentoring for the Not-Consciously-Christian

Introduction

Life Mentor Training promotes a way of assisting others who consciously identify with and are committed to Christ. However, Christian worker's value and find themselves forming relationships with people who are not so identified with Christ or who have not yet come to a point of consciously making a commitment to live their lives in relationship with Him.

The question arises of how to do life mentoring when in a helping relationship with a person who is not identified as with Christ. The life mentoring material and approach seem so blatantly and intentionally Christian, and the life mentoring goals appear so grounded in both persons (life mentor and client) being consciously Christians[71].

Taking a Step Back

It is true that the life mentoring approach is thoroughly integrated with a Christian view of the person and the person in relationship

---

[71] I am intentionally using the terms "not-consciously-Christian or consciously Christian," but not to muddy the waters and imply that there is no "all-or-nothing" about being a Christian. There are two categories: saved (Christian or born-again believer) and unsaved (non-Christian or unbeliever). However, in doing evangelism in a Western European country, it becomes apparent that coming to Christ is both a point in time and experienced as a linear process. The point in time is when God acts to regenerate the person (the new birth from above). The person may not immediately become conscious that this has happened, so there may be a process over time of coming to an understanding – to become consciously Christian. Also, both those *who are not born-again* and those *who are, but are not-yet-fully-conscious-of-it*, are here described as being not-consciously-Christian. The life mentor will have difficulty distinguishing between these two situations and will need to proceed similarly with people in both groups, because they are both not-consciously-Christian. Hence, there is a need for an adapted approach – one less overtly Christian.

with God through Christ and empowered by the Holy Spirit. Although this is true, there are broader truths that can be illuminated and will provide for the latitude to apply life mentoring to working with the not-consciously-Christian.

An approach to this application of life mentoring is to ask oneself what is common between Christians and non-Christians. Further, one can consider what concepts and principles in the life mentoring material can be described or labeled more generally. This process will clarify both what is possible to retain from the original life mentoring material and what is lost in this re-interpretation. The thoughts offered here are in the formative stage and continued consideration, application, and input will further clarify how to assist others who are not-consciously-Christian.

What is Retained When Mentoring the Not-Consciously-Christian?

The goals for life mentoring can be retained, but in a modified form. Life mentoring has **three primary life goals**. The **first** goal in life mentoring is to strengthen the here and now (real-time) relationship the other person has with God. Obviously, the not-consciously-Christian are not going to have a Christian God concept. As will become apparent throughout the revisions for unbelievers, a concept of God has to be replaced with a concept of connecting to something transcendent. In Alcoholics Anonymous, references to God are replaced with the term "higher power."[72] In adapting life mentoring

---

[72] I think it would be quite difficult to use any twelve-step related material, like *Life in Process*, if the person is unable to accept and identify with some kind of personal higher power. A higher power to connect-with is a foundational twelve-step principle.

for the not-consciously-Christian, using "higher power"[73] instead of God affords a way of retaining something that the client can connect with both as other-than-ones-self and as offering something for oneself. As well, attention can be paid to beliefs that the person has about relationships in general.

Secondly, life mentoring encourages growth in character (virtue development). This goal and its accompanying concept can be easily retained. The idea of developing character through growth in personal virtues is not unique to Christianity. In the realm of helping relationships, the value of virtues has been illuminated and elevated in its significance in the past decade by the positive psychology movement. The development of virtues and character is an acceptable outcome in personal growth or self-improvement.

In life mentoring, reaching these two aforementioned primary goals leads to accomplishing *a desired third goal*: improved personal coping and resilience. Life mentoring, as describe in its explicitly Christian form, seeks to effectively assist in bringing about, through improved relating with God and increased character formation, enhanced personal functioning. The individual is thus enabled to better manage and transcend personal issues and challenges, as well as to make positive progress in life. The question arises about whether the same goal fits when life mentoring those not-consciously-Christian, and it would seem that the answer is, "yes." Even those not in Christ are capable of improving with regard to increased coping and resilience in life. This improvement

---

[73] From a Christian perspective, we are very clear about who our higher power is (and we should disclose this to our clients), but from a more general perspective on a higher power it can be defined differently depending on the person. Here's a quote from the aaagostica website: "The Higher Power of the original 12 Steps is a spiritual idea. A Higher Power can be a God or another kind of symbol. It can be goodness, love, a friend or an idea. It can be our own intellectual curiosity. It can even be the 12-Step program itself. When we open ourselves to the power of spiritual resources, we open ourselves to an abundance of help that is beyond our comprehension. Each of us will find different powers, and those we use may change from day to day." http://aaagnostica.org/2014/03/26/step-2/

should not come as a surprise for two reasons that will be further examined in a later section: human nature and common grace.

What is Lost When Life Mentoring the Not-Consciously-Christian?

What is the downside and what are the disadvantages to doing life mentoring with the revised goals mentioned above? In other words, what is lost when taking out the references to a relationship with God, as He is known to Christians, and to the character formation process of becoming more Christ-like? Obviously, there is a world of difference and a huge loss in terms of the Gospel and salvation. This is not being minimized here or re-interpreted into some type of mere psychological or human improvement language.

The *first* goal is strengthening the here and now (real-time) relationship the other person has with God. Anything else, any other "higher power" is not really sufficiently powerful or personal. Yes, there is a form of transcendence that is built-into creation, both in the capacity of the person to reach out beyond herself and in, for example, the natural beauty of this world – a potential to connect to something more, but obviously this is limited. The relationship focus is also more limited to the life mentor's modeling and encouraging of better relatedness with others.

With regard to the *second* goal, there is a limited opportunity for the not-consciously-Christian person to experience virtue formation. The types of virtues and their definitions will not necessarily conform exactly to those that are biblically informed. The life mentor will need to navigate between his or her own perspective and the client's perspective. There cannot be a final appeal to the Bible for a corrective or authoritative reference regarding virtues and how they are to be defined. However, there can be a mutual exploration of "virtues" in order to determine if a virtue is actually one that will provide the desired outcome. The loss here is one of clear direction. Without the Bible as a reference, there is no true moral compass. However practically speaking, most not-consciously-Christian clients will likely agree with the majority of virtues that are congruent with a Christian perspective. For the person who is not only not-consciously-Christian, but also not born-again, there are the additional limitations of not being freed from the power of sin and not having the empowering of the Holy Spirit for virtue formation.

The **desired third goal** is an improved personal coping and resilience. Life mentoring, as describe in its explicitly Christian form, seeks to effectively assist in bringing about, through improved relating with God and increased character formation, enhanced personal functioning. This same goal is appropriate for unbelievers as well. Unbelievers and others not-consciously-Christian are capable of these changes and improvements. The loss when working, especially with unbelievers, is one of potential. Both believers and unbelievers are capable of personal growth and change, including improved coping and resilience. The difference in potential, with more for believers, is because of being regenerated and because of the presence of the Holy Spirit — though this potential is not fully actualized in any particular believer. Potential here means how much is ultimately possible to achieve. Therefore, because we are talking about a potential and not what is actual for all, by comparison, at any given point in time some unbelievers will have made more progress than some believers with regard to enhanced functioning.

Human Nature Constants

The above clarifications regarding the goals in life mentoring clients who are not-consciously-Christian are based on assumptions about human nature. One major assumption is that all people are both material and immaterial beings. In particular, all people have an immaterial soul. The unbeliever is also made in the image of God and as such retains a semblance of this unique image — e.g., uniquely human versus the rest of creation. Into this condition is also the experience of God's common grace in which God "sends rain on the just and the unjust." (Matthew 5:45b)

However, the striking difference (as alluded to previously) is that the believer's soul is regenerated (and justified in Christ) – made new in desires, freed from the power of sin, and strengthened by the Holy Spirit for sanctification. A believer is redeemed in soul, but still struggling with the not yet fully redeemed body. By contrast, though there is a soul within the unbeliever, it is not a redeemed soul. The unbeliever is in a state of being unredeemed both in soul and body. There is still potential for improvement in character, but again not as great a potential for growth as in the person who is born again and has the Holy Spirit. This unredeemed condition of an unbelieving client will likely become apparent while proceeding with the client though the *Life in Process* Worksheets. Though the difference between the believer and unbeliever is difficult to describe concretely, the term "lost" (as associated with those not yet saved) will make more sense experientially. There will likely be, in unbelievers, a less sharp distinction between the desires of the soul and the desires of the flesh, whereas in believers there can be a clearer distinction between godly desires of the soul and the sinful desires of the flesh.

In summary, the basic structure of human nature is the same for both those who are in-Christ and those not in Christ. As such, life mentoring can also be used to assist unbelievers to have some measure of control over and influence on changing their whole persons. The life mentoring work with people who are not-consciously-Christian is important. There is value in this helping in-and-of-itself, apart from any evangelistic potential. However, going through the process may actually become pre-evangelistic for some who will eventually come to Christ. The material provided here is not intended to in any way minimize the significance of or value of assisting others who are not-consciously-Christian, neither is it intended to devalue them as persons. It is a good thing to make life mentoring available to all who have a need and are interested in this type of relationship.

Appendix B: Detachment Steps for the Person of Influence Inside Myself

Our persons can influence our brain related reactions and beyond to the whole person. Jeffrey Schwartz has researched Obsessive Compulsive Disorder (OCD) and has written about how OCD can be self-treated by following four steps. He has generalized these steps to apply to other deceptive brain messages as well:

1. *Relabel* – Identify your deceptive brain messages and the uncomfortable sensations; call them what they really are.

2. *Reattribute* – Change your perception of the importance of the deceptive brain messages; say why these thoughts, urges, and impulses keep bothering you; they are *false brain* messages (It's not ME, it's just my BRAIN!).

3. *Refocus* – Direct your attention toward an activity or mental process that is wholesome and productive – even while the false and deceptive urges, thoughts, impulses, and sensations are still present and bothering you.

4. *Revalue* – Clearly see the thoughts, urges, and impulses for what they are, simply sensations caused by deceptive brain messages that are not true and that have little to no value (they are something to dismiss, not focus on).[74]

Life mentoring is not directly addressing psychological problems, like OCD, but the steps Schwartz outlines can be adapted for use. The immaterial person, as described in the life mentoring material, is the

---

[74] Schwartz, *You Are Not Your Brain: The 4-Step Solution for Changing Bad Habits, Ending Unhealthy Thinking, and Taking Control of Your Life*, 90-91.

one who makes the choices to manage the material brain's personal reactions and deceptive messages. Life mentors can encourage their clients to address these personal issues and reactions. For example, life mentors can remind clients of these steps, and they (their persons) can then remind themselves (the whole person). The detachment steps can be further clarified for life mentoring clients to include:

1. *In Relabeling* – that the dysfunctional and sinful reactions (malfunctions) are brain and body reactions and not who they are as a persons (though affecting the whole person).

2. *In Reattributing* – that the dysfunctional and sinful reactions are malfunctions (deceptive brain messages) in the physical brain and body.

3. *In Refocusing* – by defining these malfunctions (deceptive brain messages) as distinct from their persons (though affecting the whole person) and by making healthy, virtue-based choices instead.

4. *In Revaluing* – these malfunctions as being inconsistent with their persons and inconsistent with life management and flourishing.

The problematic issues or deceptive brain messages are not denied, but they are put in perspective by the person taking a position of detachment (distinctness of the person)/self-distancing (decentering). This position is not just an abstract idea, because the detachment position is backed-up with or grounded and strengthened by knowledge of the reality that the person is actually and structurally not the same as the brain and body. Therefore, the person is able to make choices that impact the brain and body. The regenerate person's potential for this efficacy is understood to be even greater by having been re-created – being freed from the power of sin, and being strengthened by the Holy Spirit.

Appendix C: The Challenge of Client Modes

Descriptions and Definitions

One of the challenges in our own responses to situations is that we react out of parts of our psychological selves. You might have thought to yourself or said to someone, "a part of me wants to ____ and a part of me wants to do ____," or "on the one hand, I feel ____ and on the other hand, I also feel ____." We might not realize what is happening, but these "parts" of us are just that; they are differing pieces of our psychological selves (in our brains) that get triggered or activated. One label that psychologists have given these parts is schema modes.

According to Jeffrey Young, "a schema mode is: a facet of the self, involving specific schemas or coping responses that has not been fully integrated with other facets. According to this perspective, schema modes can be characterized by the degree to which a particular schema mode state has become dissociated, or cut off, from an individual's other modes. A schema mode, therefore, is a part of the self that is cut off, to some degree, from other aspects of the self."[75]

The various modes have been organized into four categories. There are are dysfunctional child modes, the dysfunctional parent modes, dysfunctional coping modes, and the healthy modes. The following are brief descriptions of each of these types of modes:

Dysfunctional Child Modes are associated with intense negative emotions such as rage, sadness, and abandonment. They are much like the concept of an "inner child" that is described in some psychotherapies.

Dysfunctional Parent Modes is also a highly emotional mode, and it is conceptually similar to what Psychodynamic theory describes as introjects or representations of others that

---

75 "Schema Modes" accessed 5 September 2016, www.schematherapy.com/id61.htm

are psychologically taken inside a person. In this case, the dysfunctional parent responses to the child are taken-in or internalized. In the dysfunctional parent mode, for example, people keep putting pressure on themselves or hate themselves.

Dysfunctional Coping Modes are related to ways of coping with avoiding, surrendering, or over-compensating schemas (core beliefs) in the person. People in an avoidant mode, avoid emotions and other inner experiences, or avoid social contact with others. When in an over-compensating mode, people stimulate or in some way inflate (aggrandize) their own importance in order to experience the opposite of their actual schema-related emotions.

Healthy Modes are those of healthy adults and happy children. In healthy adult modes, people are able to view life and their psychological selves in a realistic way. They are able to fulfill obligations, but at the same time can care for their own needs and well-being. This is similar to the psychodynamic concept of "healthy ego functioning." The happy child mode is related to fun, joy, and play.[76]

Relevance of Modes for Life Mentoring

What does this have to do with life mentoring? Life mentors will experience their clients also shifting between their psychological parts or modes. For many people this shifting will be more like simply a change in mood, such as moving into a lonely mood or an angry mood. However, some clients will have stronger distinctions and differences between their modes, and these modes will not be as well connected to each other. The mentor might react internally to the client's shift with a sense of, "Whoa, were did that come from?" or "Wow, I didn't see that coming!" or even, "Who is this person that just appeared?". It can also be difficult for life mentors to not

---

[76] Arntz & Jacob, *Schema Therapy in Practice: An Introductory Guide to the Schema Mode Approach*, 36-37.

have a spontaneous, unfiltered negative reaction to a client who has made a rather strong and possibly abrupt shift into a different mode.

Clients can be making good progress in the life mentoring, but because of events between meetings, shift into a different mood or mode that they bring into the next meeting. This mode may not have surfaced before in the life mentoring relationship. If the mode is more extreme and less connected to other modes, the life mentoring process may be interrupted, because the person has shifted into a part of himself/herself that is less able to benefit from the mentoring. The life mentor needs to continue being relationally consistent, even though the client has shifted. This can be a challenge, because the client is not doing as well and maybe is even being difficult, or is making risky and unwise choices. If the client's mode is more extreme, counseling may be necessary.

Though the unhealthy modes can be quite powerful and disturbing, they are merely psychological. This is not to minimize the influence of modes, especially an uncontrolled influence, but to put modes into the proper perspective. Modes are not the person. Modes are in the brain's psychological functioning. Modes influence the person, because of being a whole person, but ones person (soul/spirit) is capable of influencing psychological modes. Life mentors can help clients remember that their person is not their modes, and their person can make choices (using their determinate wills). In other words, their persons (souls/spirits) are capable of influencing these brain-based psychological modes. It's additionally important to keep in mind that when clients are believers, their persons have been regenerated and are growing in virtues, they have been freed from the power of sin, and the Holy Spirit is available in them to strengthen their person to influence the brain's psychological modes.

Appendix D: Core Conditions/Attitudes in the Life Mentor

Life mentoring has a relationship focus for helping clients change. In this relationship, virtues are being communicated both by example (modeled) and by being directly taught. In order for this exchange of virtues to be accomplished, certain core conditions have to be present in the relationship. These core conditions have been widely researched.[77] The following is a description of these three basic conditions or principles that reflect the attitude of the life mentor toward the client.[78]

The Core Conditions/Attitudes

1. The life mentor is **congruent** with the client.

2. The life mentor provides the client with **positive regard**.

3. The life mentor shows **empathetic** understanding to the client.

Congruence

Congruence is also called genuineness. This means that life mentors are concerned to allow clients to experience them as they really are.

The life mentor does not have a facade, that is, the life mentor's internal and external experiences are one in the same. In short, the life mentor is authentic.

---

[77] "...the value of empathy, unconditional positive regard, and congruence is supported by the latest generation of psychotherapy process-outcome research." Kirschenbaum, The Current Status of Carl Rogers and The Person-Centered Approach, 46.

[78] This material is excerpted and adapted from: McLeod, S. A. (2015). Person Centered Therapy. Retrieved from www.simplypsychology.org/client-centred-therapy.html

Positive Regard

The next core condition is **positive regard**. It is believed that for people to grow and fulfill their potential it is important that they are valued as themselves.

This refers to the life mentor's deep and genuine caring for the client. The life mentor may not approve of some of the client's actions, but the life mentor does show acceptance toward the client's person. In short, the life mentor needs an attitude of, "I'll accept you as you are." The life mentor is thus careful to maintain a genuine positive attitude toward the client, even when in disagreement with the client's actions. (Note: Some client behavior and attitudes may need to be confronted, but timing and approach are crucial. The point here is for the life mentor to not immediately become moralistic.)

Empathy

Empathy is the ability to understand what the client is feeling. This refers to the life mentor's ability to understand sensitively and accurately (but not sympathetically) the client's experience and feelings in the here-and-now. Empathy is understanding "as if" it were the life mentor's experience, while not owning or taking-on the experience as ones own.

An important part of the task of the life mentor is to follow precisely what the client is feeling and to communicate to the client that the life mentor understands what the client is feeling.

Appendix E: Stages of Change, *Life in Process* Content, and Virtue Examples

Stages of Change[79] Correlated with *Life in Process*[80] Content and Virtue Examples

STAGE ONE: The Current Picture: Helping clients tell their story and clarify key issues — **SURRENDER TO GOD**

	Content	Virtue Example
Chapter One:	*Unmanageableness*	Awareness
Chapter Two:	*Powerlessness*	Submissive
Chapter Three:	*Belief in Someone Greater Than Myself*	Faithful
Chapter Four:	*Renewed Sanity*	Hopeful

STAGE TWO: The Preferred Picture: Helping clients choose, shape, and set viable goals — **SELF-EXAMINING WITH A KNOWING OF TRUTH**

	Content	Virtue Example
Chapter Five:	*Turning to God*	Repentant
Chapter Six:	*The Life Inventory*	Self-Examining
Chapter Seven:	*Admitting*	Honest
Chapter Eight:	*Committing and Desiring God to Remove Patterns*	Trusting
Chapter Nine:	*Humbly Asking God to Renew Our Minds*	Humble
Chapter Ten:	*Renewing Sick and Sinful Patterns*	Cooperative

---

[79] Egan, *Skilled Helper*, 35-38.
[80] Morgan, *Life in Process*.

STAGE THREE: The Way Forward: Helping clients develop strategies and plans to accomplish goals – **REWORKING/RENEWAL**

	Content	Virtue Example
Chapter Eleven:	*Transforming into Patterns of Righteousness*	Reliant
Chapter Twelve:	*Willing to Amend*	Willing
Chapter Thirteen:	*Amending*	Courageous
Chapter Fourteen:	*The Inventory Continued and Admissions Promptly Made*	Diligent
Chapter Fifteen:	*Seeking Growth with Jesus*	Open

Appendix F: Worksheet Examples

Life in Process

UNMANAGEABLENESS
Worksheet 1

Summary Points

1. 'Unmanageableness' is defined as a life that is out of control in some certain personal areas of one's life or more generally in all areas.

2. Unmanageableness can be identified by noticing areas of over-attention.

3. Unmanageableness is being demonstrated if something or someone negatively consumes large quantities of time and energy and limits the person.

4. Unmanageableness takes away from the quality of relationship with God.

5. Unmanageableness hinders trust in God.

6. When life is out of control, it is difficult to experience God's loving care.

Processing Questions

1. At what point does your life seem out of control?

2. What emotions does being out of control produce in you?

3. What do you tend to do when you get to this point?

4. What advantages are there to finally "hitting bottom" and realizing life is out of control?

5. How do you think God looks at you when your life is out of control?

6. How does this affect whether you come to Him or not?

7. In what dark rooms of your life is God beginning to turn on a light?

Characteristic God Responses

1. God sees and understands the unmanageableness.

2. God's love is extended even while life seems out of control.

3. The unmanageableness blocks the experience of God's loving care.

4. God is actively involved, even when not experienced by the person, and He is working toward exposing the reasons for the unmanageableness.

Life in Process

BELIEF IN SOMEONE GREATER THAN MYSELF
Worksheet 3

Summary Points

1. This belief in someone greater than ourselves has various aspects.

2. God is more powerful in the sense of physical strength.

3. The greater than ourselves also applies to His character: all-powerful and He is all-good.

4. Doubts about God's power and goodness (His being a loving God) undermine trust in Him.

5. When doubt is present, it is difficult to believe that God is the all-powerful and good daddy we can depend on.

6. Jesus was God's object lesson about Himself: God's live demonstration on earth.

7. God was showing Himself to us in the person of Jesus.

8. To further connect with and experience God's love, we need to have an experience of other people who love us for who we are, without conditions.

Processing Questions

1. What difficulty do you have believing in a God who is physically greater or stronger than you?

2. What questions or doubts arise for you when you think about God being good? (e.g., "What about all the suffering in the world.").

3. When is it hardest for you to believe God is all-powerful and all-good?

4. When is it especially important for you to have a God who is all-powerful and all-good?

5. Who was it that first demonstrated God's unconditional love to you?

6. How do you react when you meet someone who shows you love with no strings attached and acceptance that you don't have to earn by performing?

7. How has an unloving environment hindered you from understanding God's power and goodness?

8. Having learned something of God's unconditional love, how can you now respond to those who have been hurtful?

Characteristic God Responses

1. God is still all-powerful and all-good, even when suffering and doubt occurs.

2. God is trustworthy and dependable.

3. God's love, in Christ Jesus, is not conditional on the person's performance.

Life in Process

THE LIFE INVENTORY
Worksheet 6

Summary Points

1. There is often a resistance to remembering and looking at negative childhood events.

2. These resistances are sometimes defenses to protect us.

3. Overwhelming emotions can also cause one to retreat from taking an inventory.

4. The life inventory is a visit back to one's past.

5. A time of renewal is a time for cleansing and healing from old hurts.

6. A time of renewal is also a time to reflect on where one's life has been, both in terms of negative events, as well as the positive ones.

Processing Questions

1. What happens to you when you remember certain painful areas of your childhood?

2. Where is Jesus when you remember your past?

3. What were the following people like when you were growing up:

Father?

Mother?

Describe one or two significant relatives (e.g., siblings, aunts, uncles or grandparents).

Describe one or two people who had a major impact on you (e.g. teachers, coaches or Sunday School teachers).

4. List events (both positive and negative) that have continued to stand out in your mind, even though they occurred while you were growing up.

Characteristic God Responses

1. God understands and is patient and gracious as the person resists taking the inventory.

2. God's love is poured out into the person's heart as hurt and suffering is remembered.

3. God is always ready to reach-out, forgive, and reassure of His love and acceptance.

Life in Process

COMMITTING AND DESIRING FOR GOD TO REMOVE PATTERNS

Worksheet 8
Summary Points

1. Trust and will are two keys to unlocking a victorious, abundant Christian life.

2. People often cling to well-worn, consistently ineffective, unhealthy, destructive, recurring patterns of living.

3. An act of will is required to move out of the pain.

4. The moving out is done as one directs the will toward trusting the person of God.

5. As dearly loved children of God, Christians have an inheritance.

6. As long as there are hindrances, the person will have difficulty experiencing the inheritance.

7. Increasing awareness of the hindrances provides the person with a choice — a choice to come to freedom in Jesus.

Processing Questions

1. When you are at a point where you want God to remove unhealthy patterns of behavior or thinking, what distrustful thoughts invade your thinking?

2. What objections do you have to using your will to decide to trust God?

3. When you think of entrusting yourself more completely to God, what feelings and thoughts come up for you?

4. When you imagine an actively involved, healthy father, who hears and understands your needs, how does it feel to know He is working to remove your unhealthy patterns of behavior and thinking?

Characteristic God Responses

1. God is trustworthy.

2. God has committed to the person permanently in adoption.

3. God is responsive to the person's requests, in a way consistent with His love and perfect wisdom.

4. God is faithful and brings about the person's spiritual maturity.

Life in Process

TRANSFORMING INTO PATTERNS OF RIGHTEOUSNESS
Worksheet 11

Summary Points

1. There are two types of righteousness in the Christian life.

2. The first and most critical righteousness comes as an act of God when the person is saved — Jesus is then the person's righteousness.

3. Jesus did the work that provides the way for us to stand confidently before God.

4. God is able to accept us completely in Jesus, in regards to the righteousness in Jesus.

5. The other righteousness has to do with our performance.

6. Performance righteousness does not establish or maintain our status as children of God.

7. Performance righteousness does not earn God's acceptance.

8. Performance righteousness is, however, the result of our having the right relationships God desires for us to have with Himself, others, and ourselves.

9. Performance righteousness comes from being truly loved, and it is being truly loving.

10. Once one has done the psychological work of identifying old hindrances and humbly asking God to remove them, then there are fewer hindrances to growth as God works within.

11. This work brings the person into a more complete oneness with God.

Processing Questions

1. What does it mean to you to hear that God accepts you completely in Jesus?

2. When have you felt this type of unconditional acceptance in your relationships with others?

3. Being righteous in our performance means being more like Jesus. How successful have you been at living more righteously?

4. When your life feels unmanageable and you are unable to pull it all together, how do you think God is working in you to develop your righteousness?

5. What parts of your inner person still remain separate from God?

6. How have you experienced the separate places of your heart become more one with God and your bond deeper with him?

Characteristic God Responses

1. God is actively working for the best interest of the person, in the removal of hindrances.

2. God desires that the positive work of Christ also becomes real in theperson's life.

3. God desires that the person's performance comes-out of gratitude not fear.

4. God pursues a deeper relationship with the person, based in His complete acceptance of the person in Christ.

Appendix G: Life Goals and Situational Goals Together

This material is being presented to resolve possible confusion between the three broad and foundational goals of life mentoring, the *life goals* and the goals of the stages of change, the *situational goals*. The three *life goals* are: 1. Strengthening the here-and-now (real-time) relationship with God or use of the higher power, 2. Growth in character (virtue development), and 3. Improved personal coping and resilience. The *situational goals* are related to the client's story and are individualized. In other words, the situational goals are client specific, depending on what needs to change for the client and what the client desires for a positive outcome.

These two sets of goals are being clarified and worked-on at the same time during the life mentoring process. The *life goals* are general and are about important and foundational areas of growth for the client in order to have a more godly and/or healthy resilience in life. In a sense, they are also the foundational solution to the situational needs of the client. The *situational goals* are better resolved when progress has also being made in the life goals.

That is to say, while taking action toward changing in some practical part of the client's life, the client is becoming more able to rely on her relationship with God (or use of a higher power) and is also practicing and growing in virtues that are needed to take action. For example, if the client has offended a friend and there has been conflict, the client needs to take action to repair the relationship – to apologize and ask for the friend's forgiveness. This will be done with more confidence if the she is trusting in God's active participation with her in the restoration with her friend. As well, if she is entering into the process of restoration with more self-awareness, humility, and patience, she will be communicating more clearly, congruently, and appropriately her desire for a restored relationship. The client would be taking actions that are simultaneously flowing out of both *situational* and *life goals* that are being blended and worked-on together.

www.ingramcontent.com/pod-product-compliance
Lightning Source LLC
Chambersburg PA
CBHW072002090426
42740CB00011B/2047